CW00338809

Yes, this is the front
of the book.

To our mothers, brothers, lovers, family and friends who put up with our shit when we work so much.

An Hachette UK Company

www.hachette.co.uk

First published in Great Britain in 2016 by Mitchell Beazley, a division of Octopus Publishing Group Ltd
Carmelite House
50 Victoria Embankment
London EC4Y 0DZ

www.octopusbooks.co.uk

ISBN 978 1 78472 188 6

A CIP catalogue record for this book is available from the British Library.

Printed and bound in China.

10 9 8 7 6 5 4 3 2 1

Oven temperatures used are for conventional ovens throughout. Ovens should be preheated to the specified temperature. If using a fan-assisted oven, follow the manufacturer's instructions for adjusting the time and temperature. Grills should also be preheated.

All eggs used are medium. The Department of Health advises that eggs should not be consumed raw. This book contains some dishes made with raw or lightly cooked eggs. It is prudent for more vulnerable people such as pregnant and nursing mothers, invalids, the elderly, babies and young children to avoid uncooked or lightly cooked dishes made with eggs.

Standard level spoon measurements are used in all recipes.

Neither the authors nor the publishers take any responsibility for any injury or damage resulting from the use of techniques shown or described in this book.

Publishing Director **Stephanie Jackson**
Senior Editor **Pauline Bache**
Art Director **Juliette Norsworthy**
Photographer **Paul Winch-Furness**
Stylist **Linda Berlin**
Recipe Tester **Alice Hart**
Illustrator **Grace Helmer**
Picture Research **Giulia Hetherington and Jennifer Veall**
Senior Production Manager **Katherine Hockley**

MITCHELL BEAZLEY

Ross Shonhan & Tom Moxon

Bone Daddies ramen bar
THE COOKBOOK

CONTENTS

Introduction

Over the past few years we've developed an incredibly passionate following of people who really love what we do, which is very humbling and overwhelming. So, now that we've got plenty of happy people eating our food, Tom and I – Tom mostly – were able to dedicate some time to sharing the Bone Daddies experience.

We want to push the world of ramen outside of Japan and this is about having people participate in the Bone Daddies' experience. When we first started this journey, there was very little material available in English, so this was our chance to deliver a detailed book on ramen. We want this book to be an opportunity for people to get involved with our ramen adventures and to try some of the recipes at home. Ideally, we'd like people – professional chefs even – to take these recipes as a starting point and then add their own unique vision.

The thought of people in various parts of the world having this book in their homes, helping to spread our version of ramen is really quite incredible.

We believe that ramen is an art form and one of the greatest meals out there. It deserves a huge amount of time and care; some of these recipes involve lots of different elements and many need be started a day – or even a couple of weeks – in advance. We know that cooking in a professional kitchen is vastly different to cooking at home and there are suggestions and tips for making things easier if you are short of time. We've suggested storage instructions wherever possible and, as you get more and more into the ways of ramen, you'll find it's often worth making a big batch of a tare (ramen seasoning) or a pickle because you will use it again and again. Ultimately, we hope you find your efforts as rewarding as we have and that the first time that you serve a perfectly balanced 20-hour tonkotsu to a big table of family and friends, their happy, satisfied faces make the whole thing worthwhile.

Ross on starting Bone Daddies

When I started thinking about the idea of Bone Daddies I'd been cooking Japanese food professionally for years. I'd already been to Japan, I'd eaten ramen and I'd fallen in love with it. I'd heard stories of people around the world cooking ramen and so I started, just out of interest, reading about ramen and studying what I could. This was seven or eight years ago and there wasn't a lot in English about ramen, but I read everything I could. After this, Tom was working in a hotel in Japan, but they wouldn't let him cook Japanese food, only French. He only had a couple of months left on his visa when we met up for dinner in Japan. 'Don't just stay working there unhappily. What do you love? What do you want to learn?' And he said, 'Well, I really love ramen,' and I replied, 'Fuck, me too!' So Tom went to work in a ramen bar. He gave his services for free, but they were happy to pass on all their knowledge and recipes, and he was constantly taking notes and photos. Meanwhile, I came back to London and started looking at restaurant sites.

When we opened Bone Daddies, I'd never cooked ramen professionally and there was a freedom that came with that — we could do everything the way we wanted and we wanted to create our own style. So, while Tom and I knew a hell of a lot about the principles of ramen making and had a good understanding of the nuances of it, aside from Tom's short time working at that ramen bar in Japan, we hadn't actually done it in a professional environment at all.

In principle, I knew the basics. I knew how to extract flavour from bones after all the years of cooking that I'd done, but there are some very big differences. European stocks you simmer because you want clean sauces, whereas you boil the shit out of ramen stocks because all you care about is flavour. There are so many instances like that, where Japanese cooking differs wildly from European methods. However, I knew we could extract flavour from bones, I knew how to season soups, I knew how to cook the toppings, and I had ideas for the different flavour ramen we were going to make. So I decided to risk my life savings, found investment and opened a noodle bar. I was shitting myself.

Our food

In contrast to many ramen bars in Japan, the menu at Bone Daddies is pretty varied and complex. When we were developing our menu, we knew straightaway that we had to serve more than one soup, to cater for people who don't eat pork or chicken, for example. So we had three, sometimes four, different stocks at any one time. We wanted to take this further by pairing a specific stock with a specific tare and a specific topping. This means that when you visit Bone Daddies and order from our menu, you end up ordering a particular composition. Most bowls of ramen in Japan have three or four toppings but we'll sometimes have six or seven and, because we're experienced chefs, we often got carried away with the fun of it and ended up delivering a uniquely 'London' ramen experience. So we ended up making our ramen kitchen more complicated than in Japan.

We've really pushed the variety at Bone Daddies and the idea is that ramen is constantly evolving so, while we have ramen representative of Japan's north, south and Tokyo, we've also got unique recipes that only we make.

Moving forward, we're almost going back to basics in some areas. As we continue to develop ramen, we've been stripping away some of the more involved elements. Some of the early, complicated recipes are still the most popular on the menu, but we're also taking some back to their purest form. Because, in the restaurant business, if you're not pushing forwards, you can only be going backwards. So you have to be intensely critical of your thought processes and we're always questioning how we do things.

www.bonedaddies.com

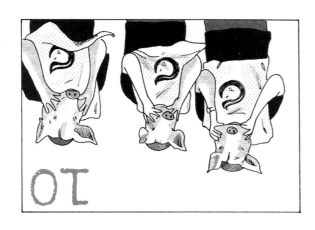

10

Globe Artichokes with Green Chilli Mayo

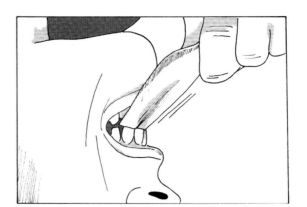

In season, a simple boiled artichoke is a beautiful thing. Pulling off the petals, working your way to the heart — which is like a prize for your efforts — is social and fun. This is a very European vegetable that also embodies the food served at *izakayas* in Japan. It is strange how many people order it but don't know how to get to the heart, so we teach them how to do it along the way, which is great!

Serves 2

2 large globe artichokes, stalks trimmed

130g Green Chilli Mayo (see right)

Green Chilli Mayo (makes 130g, enough for 2 generous servings)

90g Hellmann's mayonnaise

2 tablespoons Green Chilli Ginger Dressing (see page 70)

1 tablespoon Orange Ponzu (see page 44)

1. To make the Green Chilli Mayo, mix all the ingredients together in a bowl. The mayo will keep in an airtight container in the refrigerator for up to 5 days.

2. Simmer the globe artichokes, uncovered, in a saucepan of water for about 30 minutes, until the outer leaves can be easily pulled away. Drain, then plunge into iced water for 10 minutes. Drain well, squeezing out the excess water.

3. Cut each artichoke in half top to bottom and serve with the mayo.

Cabbage & Miso

. . . .

A lot of people think Japan's restaurants are all quite formal and sterile, but *izakayas* are very simple pub-style venues where uncomplicated foods are served alongside the drinks. In the same way as nuts would be served in many Western bars, in one visit to an *izakaya* we were handed bowls of large chunks of green cabbage with a smear of delicious *shiro* (white) miso – the simplicity was perfect. Here is our version.

Serves 4

1 small Hispi (sweetheart or pointed) cabbage, chilled

1¾ tablespoons shiro (white) miso

2 teaspoons akadashi (red) miso

½ tablespoon caster sugar

Miso Dipping Sauce

2 tablespoons moromi miso

2 tablespoons mugi (barley) miso

1. To make the Miso Dipping Sauce, mix all the ingredients together well in a bowl with 2 tablespoons of water until the sugar has dissolved.

2. Cut the chilled cabbage into 6 wedges from tip to base. Trim off the hard stalk at the base of each wedge and gently separate each of the layers, but keep the wedges intact.

3. Serve with the dipping sauce on the side.

17

Green Bean Salad with Barley Miso Lime Dressing

A very simple spring vegetable salad with an easy dressing, this is a light, refreshing option to complement a bowl of ramen in warmer weather.

Serves 4

2 globe artichokes, stalks trimmed

120g green beans, topped and tailed

150g sugar snap peas, topped and tailed, strings removed

40g petits pois

8 fine asparagus spears, woody bases trimmed

4 pak choi hearts, cut into bite-sized pieces

120ml Barley Miso Lime Dressing (see right)

Barley Miso Lime Dressing
(makes 275ml)

80g mugi (barley) miso

75ml rice wine vinegar

25g honey

50ml vegetable oil

10ml ginger juice, squeezed from finely grated fresh root ginger

¼ teaspoon finely grated lime zest

25ml lime juice (from 1 large lime)

1 teaspoon sesame oil

1. To prepare the Barley Miso Lime Dressing, put the barley miso, vinegar, honey, vegetable oil and ginger juice into a blender and blitz until smooth. (Alternatively, whisk together by hand in a bowl.) Stir in the lime zest and juice and sesame oil. Cover and chill in the refrigerator before using.

2. Simmer the globe artichokes, uncovered, in a saucepan of water for about 30 minutes, until the outer leaves can be easily pulled away. Drain, then plunge into iced water for 10 minutes. Drain well, squeezing out the excess water. Carefully remove the outer leaves (which can be eaten separately), the tough inner leaves and the hairy choke and discard. Cut the soft artichoke heart into bite-sized pieces.

3. Bring a large saucepan of water to the boil. Add the green beans, sugar snaps, petits pois and asparagus to the pan, set a timer and blanch for 1 minute 50 seconds.

4. Add the pak choi pieces and cook for a further 10 seconds, then drain, plunge into iced water and drain well.

5. Cut each asparagus spear into thirds. Arrange the salad ingredients in serving bowls and gently toss with the chilled dressing.

18

Heirloom Tomato Salad

Summer on a plate, this is one of our favourite dishes.
It shows off beautiful tomatoes with delicate Japanese flavours.

Serves 3

500g heirloom tomatoes, chilled and cut into 2cm pieces

large pinch of Maldon sea salt

90ml Hiyashi Chuka (see page 204)

1 teaspoon Chilli Oil (see page 104)

1 teaspoon sesame oil

1 teaspoon Mayu (see page 104)

1¼ teaspoons finely sliced garlic shoots

1¼ teaspoons Garlic Chips (see page 128)

1. Season the tomatoes with the sea salt and mix well in a bowl. Divide between chilled serving plates.

2. Sprinkle the remaining ingredients on top of the tomatoes, finishing with the Garlic Chips, and serve.

Tenderstem Broccoli with Yuzu Koshō Mayo

A lot of people love broccoli and many more would happily drink this dressing. Put the two together and you have a great dish to eat before, or with, a bowl of ramen.

Serves 4

400g Tenderstem broccoli
160g Yuzu Koshō Mayo (see right)

Yuzu Koshō Mayo (makes 200g)

60ml (4 tablespoons) Orange Ponzu (see page 44)
120g Hellmann's mayonnaise
25g yuzu koshō

1. To make the Yuzu Koshō Mayo, mix the Orange Ponzu, mayo and yuzu koshō together in a bowl very thoroughly.

2. Blanch the broccoli in a saucepan of boiling water for 2 minutes, refresh in iced water, then drain. Trim the stems and remove any remaining leaves.

3. Serve the broccoli with the mayo on the side.

Edamame with Sweet Spicy Soy Sauce

Because we don't want to serve just plain edamame with salt.

Sweet Spicy Soy Sauce
(makes about 330ml)

130ml Japanese soy sauce

1 tablespoon sesame oil

160g caster sugar

2 tablespoons kochujan
– MSG-free is best

2 tablespoons Chilli Bits
(see page 129)

3 garlic cloves, puréed
with a little of the soy
sauce

Edamame (per serving)

130g frozen edamame, in
their pods

3 tablespoons Sweet Spicy
Soy Sauce (see left)

1. To make the Sweet Spicy Soy Sauce, combine the soy sauce, sesame oil and sugar in a saucepan and bring to the boil. Remove from the heat, then whisk in the kochujan, Chilli Bits and garlic purée. This will keep in the refrigerator for up to 2 weeks.

2. Blanch the edamame in boiling water for 2 minutes. Drain and serve hot straight away, with the sauce on the side.

Simmered Pumpkin

We love *kabocha* squash. This dish is very much like the simmered *kabocha* dishes you find in Japan.

Serves 5

Pickled Shishito Peppers (makes about 100g)

100ml rice wine vinegar

20g caster sugar

100g shishito or Padrón peppers, shredded into 2mm-thick slices

Simmered Pumpkin

2 small Japanese pumpkins (kabocha), about 1kg each

300ml Soy Tare (see page 108)

150ml mirin

Dressing (makes 225ml)

150ml pumpkin cooking liquid, reserved from making the Simmered Pumpkin (see left)

75ml shishito pickling liquid, reserved from making the Pickled Shishito Peppers (see left)

To Serve (per serving)

8-10 pieces Simmered Pumpkin (see left)

6 tablespoons Dressing (see left)

15g Pickled Shishito Peppers (see left)

pinch of toasted white sesame seeds

large pinch of kizami nori (sliced nori)

1. To make the Pickled Shishito Peppers, bring the vinegar and sugar to the boil and add the peppers. Take off the heat and leave to cool, then strain, reserving the liquid for the dressing.

2. To prepare the pumpkins, cut in half from top to bottom. Using a spoon, scoop out the seeds and soft flesh from the inside. Cut each half in half again. Trim away the tough stalks and base parts, then cut the unpeeled pumpkins into evenly sized triangular wedges about 4cm across. Using a small paring knife, remove all the sharp-angled edges from each piece of pumpkin – this not only looks good but facilitates the even cooking of each piece.

3. Place the prepared pumpkin in a small saucepan and cover with the Soy Tare, mirin and 900ml water. Simmer gently over a low heat for about 30 minutes, or until the pumpkin is just soft through to the centre. Remove from the heat and leave the pumpkin to cool completely in the liquid, then cover and refrigerate.

4. To make the dressing, mix the ingredients together well in a bowl.

5. To serve, add all the ingredients to a chilled bowl and serve immediately.

Pickled Shiitake

We boil a lot of dried shiitake to make our mushroom stock, so we came up with the idea to pickle them. The first attempt made us think of some similar Sichuan dishes we've had. So we dressed it with our chilli oil and some fresh leek for texture and freshness.

Pickling Liquid (makes about 400ml)

15g dried shiitake mushrooms

100ml light soy sauce

150ml rice wine vinegar

40g caster sugar

1 large green chilli, halved (add more if you like a bit more of a kick)

20g fresh root ginger, roughly chopped

To Serve (per serving)

4–5 shiitake mushrooms, from making the Pickling Liquid (see left), squeezed a little and chopped

3 tablespoons Pickling Liquid (see left)

1 tablespoon sesame oil

1 tablespoon Chilli Oil (see page 104)

1 shiso leaf

10g leek, trimmed and very finely chopped

pinch of toasted white sesame seeds

1. Combine the dried shiitake and 400ml of boiling water in a saucepan and simmer for 1 hour. Drain, reserving the shiitake and liquid.

2. To make the Pickling Liquid, place the reserved liquid with all the ingredients (except the reserved shiitake) in a saucepan and mix together well. Remove the stems and add the mushrooms to the liquid. Simmer for 1½ hours.

3. Remove from the heat and leave to cool, then strain, reserving the mushrooms and pickling liquid.

4. To serve, mix together the shiitake, pickling liquid, sesame oil and Chilli Oil in a bowl. Transfer to a large white ramekin and top with the shiso leaf and leek. Add the sesame seeds and serve.

If you've made Mushroom Broth (see page 101) then use 280ml Mushroom Broth and shiitake from the broth-making in place of dried and soaked shiitake.

Home-made Pickles

We had to have some pickles on the menu at Bone Daddies to eat with a ramen. We started with six or seven different veggies. The team got excited by pickles over the years and we have had up 14 different fruit and veg on a plate. They are great to have on the table with drinks as well as for eating during and after a ramen.

Kimchi

Makes 750g

140g fine table salt
3 Chinese cabbages, each cut into 8 wedges

Kimchi Marinade
2 tablespoons light soy sauce
2 small garlic cloves, peeled
1 green apple, peeled, cored and roughly chopped
5g fresh root ginger, peeled and roughly chopped
60g (½ small) white onion, roughly chopped

2 tablespoons Korean chilli powder
1 tablespoon caster sugar
60g piece daikon, peeled and roughly chopped
2 tablespoons fish sauce (Squid brand)
4 spring onions, cut into 1.5cm lengths

1. Mix the salt with 2 litres of water in a bowl or sturdy container until dissolved. Submerge the cabbage in the brine, cover with a saucer and place a food can on top to weight the cabbage down, then leave in a cool place for 48 hours.

2. Now check the cabbage – it should be soft and a little salty. If it is too salty, rinse under cold running water and then leave to drain for 30 minutes.

3. Once ready, carefully trim away the hard base of each wedge (you can reserve this for making Kimchi Tare or IP Sauce with Chashu, see pages 112 and 138) and cut the cabbage into 3cm squares to serve.

4. Put the Kimchi Marinade ingredients, except the spring onion, in a blender and blend to a paste. Work the marinade paste and spring onion thoroughly into the cabbage pieces, then weight down as before and seal the bowl or container with cling film. Store in the refrigerator for at least 2 weeks before eating.

5. The Kimchi can be stored in an airtight sterilized jar in the refrigerator for up to 1 month. Be sure to loosen the lid regularly, especially when the jar is out of the refrigerator, to prevent gases building up in the jar. After 1 month, whether the Kimchi is still good to eat is a matter of personal taste. It will continue to ferment slowly and the sour flavour will deepen. At this stage, you may find it more palatable to cook with the Kimchi instead of eating it as a straight pickle. When the sourness is too much, or begins to taste 'off' to you, move on to a fresh batch of Kimchi.

Cauliflower Pickle

Makes about 275g

30g honey
½ tablespoon Maldon sea salt
30g caster sugar

½ teaspoon black peppercorns
1 fresh bay leaf
185ml rice wine vinegar

½ cauliflower (or Romanesco or purple cauliflower), trimmed and cut into bite-sized pieces (about 225g prepared weight)

1. Combine the honey, salt, sugar, peppercorns, bay leaf and vinegar with 150ml of water in a saucepan and bring just to the boil. Remove from the heat and leave to cool.

2. Add the cauliflower pieces to the cooled pickling liquid in a bowl. Leave to pickle in the refrigerator for 8 hours or overnight before serving. This will keep in the pickling liquid for up to 2 weeks.

Persimmon Pickle

Makes about 475g

250ml sushi vinegar
650ml rice wine vinegar
130g caster sugar
pared zest of ¼ orange, cut into fine julienne
25g fine table salt
3cm piece of konbu
4-5 unripe persimmons

1. Combine all the ingredients except the persimmons in a saucepan and bring just to the boil. Remove from the heat and leave to cool.

2. Using a sharp knife, pare the skin from the persimmons. Slice the stalk end from each fruit and cut the remainder into 8 segments from top to bottom.

3. Add the persimmons to the cool pickling liquid, then cover and chill in the refrigerator for 8 hours before using. This will keep in the pickling liquid for up to 3 days.

Korean Daikon Pickle

Makes about 250g

40g fine table salt
250g daikon, peeled and cut into batons about 4.5cm long x 8mm thick
250ml rice wine vinegar
½ teaspoon finely grated fresh root ginger
¼ teaspoon finely grated garlic
75g caster sugar
½ teaspoon Korean chilli powder

1. Mix the salt with 1 litre of water in a bowl. Add the daikon to the brine and leave in a cool place for 3 hours until soft and a little salty.

2. Meanwhile, combine the vinegar, ginger, garlic, sugar and chilli powder in a saucepan and bring just to the boil. Simmer for 5 minutes to infuse the flavours, then remove from the heat and leave to cool.

3. Rinse and drain the daikon and add it to the vinegar mixture. Leave to pickle in the refrigerator for a minimum of 8 hours. This will keep in the pickling liquid for up to 2 weeks.

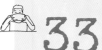

Carrot Pickle

Makes about 375g

½ teaspoon coriander seeds
½ teaspoon black peppercorns
400ml rice wine vinegar
125g caster sugar

1 tablespoon fine table salt
7cm piece dried konbu
400g carrots, peeled and cut into batons about 5cm long x 5mm thick

1. Tie the coriander seeds and peppercorns in a square of muslin into a bundle. Place in a saucepan with the vinegar, sugar, salt and konbu and bring just to the boil. Remove from the heat and leave to cool.

2. Add the carrot batons to the cooled pickling liquid. Leave to pickle in the refrigerator for 24 hours before serving. This will keep in the pickling liquid for up to 2 weeks.

Beetroot Pickle

Makes about 190g

175ml cider vinegar
50g caster sugar
1 teaspoon fine table salt
½ teaspoon Sichuan peppercorns
100g (4 medium) beetroot, any colour (pickle different colours separately), peeled and cut into batons about 5cm long x 5mm thick

1. Combine all the ingredients except the beetroot in a saucepan, pour in 50ml of water and bring just to the boil. Remove from the heat and leave to cool.

2. Add the beetroot batons to the cooled pickling liquid. Leave to pickle in the refrigerator for 8 hours or overnight before serving. This will keep in the pickling liquid for up to 2 weeks.

Bean Sprout Pickle

Makes about 85g

150g bean sprouts
1 tablespoon fine table salt
½ tablespoon rice wine vinegar
½ teaspoon caster sugar
a few drops of sesame oil
pinch of fine Korean chilli powder

1. Mix the bean sprouts with the salt in a bowl. Continue to mix every 15 minutes for 45 minutes. Transfer to a sieve and rinse thoroughly under cold running water to remove most of the salty taste.

2. Mix the vinegar, sugar, sesame oil and chilli powder together, then stir the mixture into the bean sprouts and they are ready to serve. These can only be stored in the refrigerator for about 3 days but after that they will start to turn very soft.

Nashi Pickle

Makes about 250g

1 tablespoon fine table salt
2 nashi pears
200ml Dashi (see page 108)

3cm piece of dried konbu
20g honey
2 tablespoons caster sugar
2 teaspoons Maldon sea salt

2 tablespoons rice wine vinegar
75ml pink grapefruit juice
4 teaspoons lemon juice

1. Mix the salt with 400ml of water in a bowl. To prepare the pears, top and tail each one, then scoop out the cores with a teaspoon. Slice each pear in half, then cut into 2mm-thick slices. Add to the brine and leave in a cool place for 30 minutes.

2. Drain the pear slices through a sieve and rinse thoroughly under cold running water, then pat dry with kitchen paper.

3. Combine the Dashi, konbu, honey, sugar, salt, vinegar and grapefruit and lemon juices in a saucepan and bring just to the boil. Remove from the heat and leave to cool.

4. Add the pear slices to the cooled pickling liquid in a bowl. Leave to pickle in the refrigerator for 8 hours or overnight before serving. This will keep in the pickling liquid for up to 2 weeks.

Daikon Pickle

Makes about 400g

40g fine table salt
500g daikon, peeled and cut into wedges

225ml rice wine vinegar
125g caster sugar

1. Mix the salt with 1 litre of water in a bowl. Add the daikon to the brine and leave in a cool place for 3 hours until soft and a little salty.

2. Combine 250ml of water with the vinegar and sugar in a saucepan and bring just to the boil. Remove from the heat and leave to cool.

3. Drain the daikon through a sieve and rinse thoroughly under cold running water. Add the daikon to the cooled pickling liquid in a bowl. Leave to pickle in the refrigerator for 8 hours or overnight before serving. This will keep in the pickling liquid for up to 2 weeks.

Cucumber Pickle

Makes about 200g

200ml rice wine vinegar
40g caster sugar
50g fine table salt
3cm piece of dried konbu
1 cucumber, halved
lengthways and seeds
scraped out

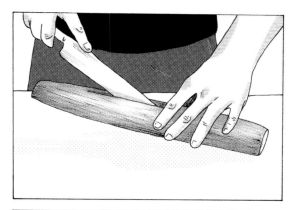

1. Place the vinegar, sugar, one-quarter of the salt and the konbu in a saucepan and bring just to the boil. Remove from the heat and leave to cool.

2. Put the cucumber in a sieve, sprinkle evenly with the remaining salt and leave to drain for 30 minutes. Hold the sieve under cold running water to rinse off the salt thoroughly, then tip the cucumber on to kitchen paper to dry.

3. Wash well until just a gentle salt taste remains. Dry and cut into wedges.

4. Add the cucumber to the cooled pickling liquid in a bowl. Leave to pickle in the refrigerator for 8 hours or overnight before serving. This will keep in the pickling liquid for up to 3 days.

Serving the Home-made Pickles

We simply arrange a mixture of the chilled pickles attractively on a plate, but here are some rough measurements.

50g Kimchi
15g Bean sprout Pickle
10g Korean Daikon Pickle
pinch Carrot Pickle

pinch of yellow Beetroot Pickle
pinch of red Beetroot Pickle
15g Cauliflower Pickle

15g Persimmon Pickle
10g Nashi Pickle
12g Daikon Pickle
12g Cucumber Pickled

Bean Sprout
Pickle

Daikon
Pickle

Kimchi

Cucumber
Pickle

Nashi
Pickle

Beetroot
Pickle

Cauliflower
Pickle

Carrot
Pickle

Persimmon
Pickle

Korean
Daikon

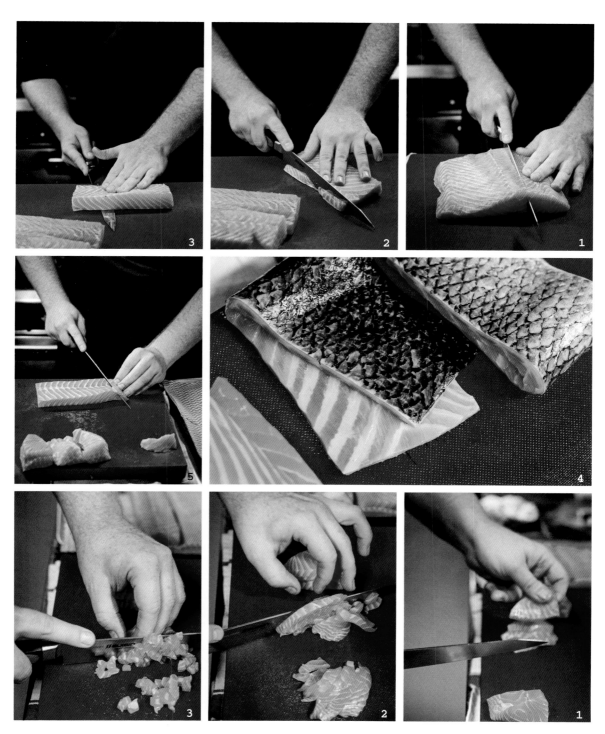

Salmon Sashimi with Shiso & Lime Soy

Salmon sashimi is not very popular in Japan, however in the West it is consistently one of the most-ordered sashimi. We created this as a simple, clean dish that could be enjoyed before a ramen. Light and easy to prepare, it hits the spot.

After you have skinned the salmon, make sure you remove any scales that remain on your knife and chopping board.

Serves 4-6

200-300g sushi-grade salmon, skin on

20-30 red shiso cress leaves

8-10g bubu arare (mini rice crackers), crushed

Lime Soy Dressing (makes 175ml)

125ml soy sauce

12ml yuzu juice

40ml lime juice

3 green shiso leaves, finely chopped

1. To make the Lime Soy Dressing, combine all the ingredients except the shiso in a bowl, cover and chill in the refrigerator until ready to serve.

2. To prepare the salmon, lay skin side down and remove the skin by running a sharp knife along the length of the block just above but not too close to the skin. The salmon can then be sliced into 4mm-thick slices (about 10g each slice), using long, smooth cuts. Chill in the refrigerator until ready to serve.

3. To serve, mix the chopped shiso leaves with the dressing and keep chilled. Lay 5 salmon slices per serving on an ice-cold serving plate and spoon about 2 tablespoons of the dressing over each serving (ensuring that each piece of salmon gets some of the chopped shiso). Place a shiso cress leaf on each salmon slice and sprinkle with the bubu arare. Serve immediately.

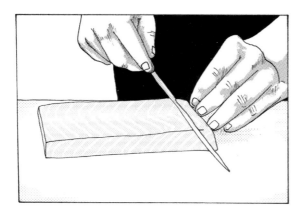

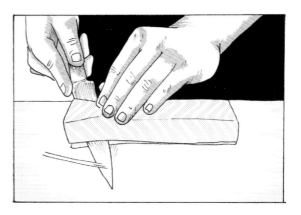

Salmon & Yellowtail Tartare with Lime Wasabi Ponzu

A tasty little starter that is easy to make and works well with a few drinks before a ramen.

Lime Wasabi Ponzu (makes 155ml)

125ml Orange Ponzu (see page 44)

25ml yuzu juice

½ teaspoon finely chopped or grated lime zest

½ teaspoon finely chopped or grated lemon zest

1 teaspoon wasabi paste

juice of ¼ lime

Lotus Chips (makes 4 servings)

1 small, fresh raw lotus root, peeled and trimmed (about 250g prepared weight)

1 lemon, halved

1 litre rapeseed or other flavourless oil, for deep-frying

shichimi togarashi, to taste

fine table salt, to taste

Tartare (per serving)

40g skinned (see page 40) sushi-grade salmon, cut into 5mm dice and chilled

15g skinned sushi-grade yellowtail (hamachi), cut into 5mm dice and chilled

1 red shiso cress leaf

2 teaspoons Lime Wasabi Ponzu – we serve ours in a pipette

6 Lotus Chips (see left)

1. To make the Lime Wasabi Ponzu, mix all the ingredients together in a bowl, cover and chill in the refrigerator until ready to serve.

2. To make the Lotus Chips, use a mandoline with a hand guard or a very sharp knife to cut the lotus widthways into 1mm-thick slices. Transfer to a bowl and immediately cover with cold water. Squeeze in the juice from the lemon halves and leave to soak for 15 minutes. Once soaked, drain the lotus slices and rinse under cold running water for a few minutes, then drain and dry very thoroughly with kitchen paper.

3. Pour the oil into a wide, deep saucepan (at least 2 litres in capacity) and set over a medium heat. When the oil reaches 140°C on a thermometer, deep-fry the lotus slices, in small batches, removing from the oil just before they become golden and draining well. Spread the lotus chips out on kitchen paper and, while they are still hot, season lightly with the shichimi and salt. Leave to cool; they should be crisp and light.

4. To serve, arrange the salmon on an ice-cold serving plate in a neat mound and top with the yellowtail. Garnish with the shiso and serve the ponzu and lotus chips on the side.

When dicing the salmon and yellowtail, keep hand contact to a minimum, as this will warm the fish and negatively affect its texture. Make sure you keep the fish chilled until ready to eat and serve on an ice-cold plate.

Pickled
Shiitake

Salmon &
Yellowtail
Tartare

Salmon Sashimi
with Shiso &
Lime Soy

Lotus Chips

Yellowtail Sashimi with Chilli, Ponzu & Coriander

Made famous by Nobu and always in demand, yellowtail sashimi with chilli is now a classic.

Serves 1

50g sushi-grade yellowtail (hamachi)

2 teaspoons Orange Ponzu (see right)

5 coriander leaves

5 slices of green chilli

Orange Ponzu (makes about 350ml)

1 tablespoon sake

1 tablespoon rice wine vinegar

1 tablespoon tamari

110ml soy sauce

40ml mirin

125ml lemon juice, strained

40ml orange juice, strained

2cm piece of dried konbu

10g katsuo bushi (bonito flakes)

¼ orange, cut into 1cm-thick slices

1. To make the Orange Ponzu, pour the sake into a saucepan and heat gently, then carefully ignite with a match or lighter to burn off the alcohol. Add the vinegar, tamari, soy sauce, mirin, lemon and orange juices and the konbu and heat to just below boiling point (90°C on a thermometer). Remove from the heat and add the bonito flakes and the orange slices. Cover and leave to infuse in the refrigerator for at least 24 hours, then strain. This will keep in a sealed container in the refrigerator for up to a month.

2. To prepare the yellowtail, remove the red centre blood line and bones to create 2 large fillets. Cut each fillet lengthways to create 4 sashimi blocks. Remove the skin as tightly to the flesh as possible. Cut each block into 5 x 4mm-thick slices.

3. To serve, place the yellowtail slices on an ice-cold serving plate and cover with the ponzu. Top each slice with a coriander leaf and a slice of chilli. Serve immediately.

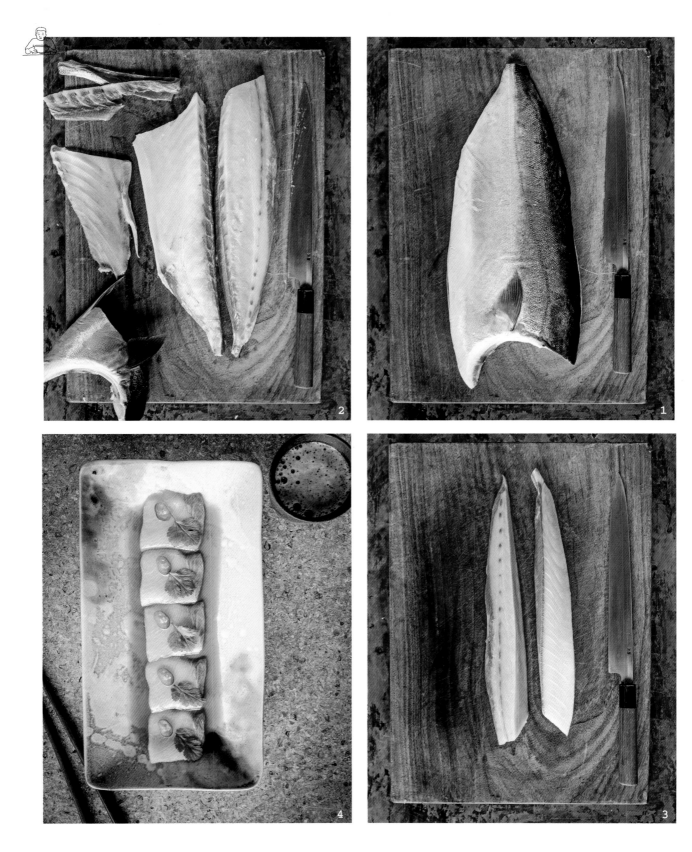

Tuna Duo (Tuna Tartare & Tataki) with Rice Crackers

A good tartare of any meat or fish is beautiful. The rice crackers are a great way to use up any leftover rice.

Serves 5

Fried Rice Crackers (makes 5 servings)

105g cooked good-quality Japanese rice

30g (about 1 large) egg white

¼ tablespoon Maldon sea salt

aonori (seaweed flakes), for sprinkling

4 litres rapeseed or other flavourless oil, for deep-frying

Tuna Tataki (makes 5 servings)

500g sushi-grade yellowfin tuna, half reserved (including trimmings) for making the Tuna Tartare (see right)

2 tablespoons vegetable oil

Maldon sea salt, to taste

freshly ground black pepper, to taste

Tuna Tartare (makes 5 servings)

250g yellowfin tuna, reserved from making the Tuna Tataki (see left)

1 small egg yolk, stirred

1 tablespoon extra virgin olive oil

1 tablespoon finely chopped white onion, soaked in cold water for 15 minutes, then rinsed and patted dry

2 teaspoons mixed black and white toasted sesame seeds

1 tablespoon Orange Ponzu (see page 44)

2 teaspoons yuzu juice

Maldon sea salt, crushed, to taste

To Serve (per serving)

50g Tuna Tataki (see left)

shichimi togarashi, to taste

50g Tuna Tartare (see left)

1 bamboo leaf, to garnish

a little kizami nori (sliced nori), finely chopped to make shorter

sushi ginger, finely sliced, to taste

40ml Orange Ponzu (see page 44)

generous handful of Fried Rice Cracker pieces (see left)

Continued

SNACKS

Tuna Duo (Tuna Tartare & Tataki) with Rice Crackers (continued)

1. To make the Fried Rice Crackers (prepare this in advance), preheat the oven to its lowest setting (You may need to prop the door open a little to reduce the temperature.) Place the rice, egg white, sea salt and 2 tablespoons of water in a powerful blender (a bar-style blender works best) and blend until completely smooth, scraping down the sides of the bowl occasionally.

2. Spread the mixture out on a large non-stick silicone baking mat, making sure that it is evenly spread. It should be about 3mm thick. Sprinkle with a layer of aonori and place in the oven for 2–3 hours. The cracker needs to be completely dry, so you may need to carefully flip it over after around 2 hours and return to the oven until it is no longer flexible.

3. If you have time, after the oven drying you can continue slowly drying the cracker at room temperature until ready to use.

4. Pour the oil into a large, deep saucepan (at least 4 litres in capacity) and set over a medium-high heat. Break the cracker into small pieces (about 6 x 6cm), as it will expand significantly when fried. When the oil temperature reaches 160°C on a thermometer, deep-fry the cracker pieces, 1–2 pieces only at a time, for a matter of a few seconds without colouring, flipping once during the process. It will puff up a lot. Remove with a slotted spoon and drain thoroughly on kitchen paper. Leave to cool completely and store in an airtight container.

5. To make the Tuna Tataki (again, prepare this in advance), cut the tuna into 2 'tataki blocks' about 5cm across x 3cm deep and as long as possible. The tataki blocks should weigh 250g in total (5 portions). Set the remaining tuna (including any trimmings) aside for the tartare.

6. Gently massage the oil into all sides of the tataki blocks and season really well. Heat a heavy-based frying pan over a high heat. Once it starts to smoke, quickly sear the tuna blocks on all sides – if the pan is really hot, they should only need a maximum of 5 seconds per side. Chill the seared blocks in the refrigerator for 30 minutes to firm up the flesh ready for slicing.

7. Using a very sharp knife, cut the tuna into 5mm-thick slices widthways. Refrigerate until ready to serve.

8. Just before serving, prepare the Tuna Tartare. Using a spoon, scrape away and discard any sinew from the reserved tuna. Then use a sharp knife to very finely chop the tuna until it is not quite a purée. In a bowl over ice, fold in the egg yolk and olive oil, mixing as little and as gently as possible – you need to avoid creating a mayonnaise-like consistency. Add all the remaining tartare ingredients, mixing and folding as little as necessary, and adjusting the seasoning to taste.

9. To serve, arrange the tataki slices on an ice-cold plate and sprinkle with as much shichimi as you dare. Place the tartare with the bamboo-leaf garnish in a chilled small ramekin and top with the kizami nori. Serve with the sushi ginger, Orange Ponzu and fried Rice Cracker pieces on the side.

Duck Breast Ham with Persimmon Pickle

We love curing meats and wanted to take traditional European methods and introduce miso into the mix. It was a slow process because you only know after several weeks how any batch has turned out, before you can think about changing it. We believe we got it right using our spicy miso tare, but humidity and temperature play a big part in this, so you will need some experimenting in your environment if you want to try it yourself. Duck and persimmon are both symbolic Japanese autumn foods, so they go well together.

Serves 8

4 duck breasts
200g Spicy Miso Tare (see page 109), plus 70g

70g Chilli Bits (see page 129), drained overnight, then squeezed to remove any remaining oil
¼ teaspoon Maldon sea salt

To serve

Persimmon Pickle (see page 32, pictured overleaf)
shiso leaves (optional)
orange zest (optional)

1. Carefully remove most of the sinew from the flesh side of each duck breast, being careful not to waste any of the breast meat. Using a sharp knife, carefully score the skin side of each breast lengthways, just down to the flesh. Rub some of the 200g Spicy Miso Tare over each breast, working it into the score lines.

2. Use the remainder of the 200g quantity of Spicy Miso Tare to layer the duck breasts into an airtight container and leave to marinate in the refrigerator for 68 hours.

3. Once the marinating time is up, blitz the Chilli Bits in a blender until ground (but they don't need to be very finely ground), then add the 70g of tare and the salt and blend again to mix well.

4. Wipe any excess tare from each duck breast and rub with a good coating of the chilli, tare and salt mixture. Don't make the layer too thick though as the duck needs to dry out – you may have some left over.

5. Wrap each duck breast in a piece of muslin, squeezing (not folding!) into a fat, rounded shape, rather than a thin, pointed shape. This makes it easier to slice. Hang the duck breasts

for 2–3 weeks in a cool dry place with a source of fresh air (we hang them above an ice machine at the restaurant, but the temperature should be below 18°C). Check the duck regularly: with clean hands, open up the wrapping, the surface should not be wet and you should be able to observe a gradual drying and firming process with each check. If you can't see it drying out, move the duck to a dryer, cooled, better ventilated spot (the recipe won't work in summer unless you have a controlled environment). Getting the correct temperature and humidity is important because essentially you are allowing nature to take its course, only in a controlled manner. Once they are firm and look well dried and cured, they are ready for use.

6. Remove the muslin and wrap tightly in cling film. This will keep for a month in the refrigerator.

7. To serve, cut each cured duck breast into slices, allowing half a breast per person, and arrange on serving plates with a few pieces of Persimmon Pickle and some shiso leaves on top, if liked.

Beef Tataki with Crispy Kale & Yuzu Miso Dressing

Elia, one of our chefs, created this dish for our menu. It works really well and the dressing could also be used on any other salad.

Chilli Lime Salt (makes about 100g)

90g Maldon sea salt

2 teaspoons shichimi togarashi

pinch of dried red chilli flakes

finely grated zest of ½ lime (no white pith)

Yuzu Miso Dressing (makes about 100ml)

60g Spicy Miso Tare (see page 109)

1 tablespoon yuzu juice

3 tablespoons rice wine vinegar

1 tablespoon Chilli Oil (see page 104)

1 teaspoon caster sugar

Beef and Kale (per serving)

70g picanha or other tender-cut beef, fat and sinew removed

large pinch of Chilli Lime Salt (see left)

1 litre rapeseed or other flavourless oil, for deep-frying, plus 1 teaspoon for searing the beef

small handful (about 15g) curly kale, tough stalks removed

2 tablespoons Yuzu Miso Dressing (see left)

1 small wedge of Daikon Pickle (see page 34)

toasted white sesame seeds, to serve

1. To make Chilli Lime Salt, place all the ingredients in a small food processor and briefly pulse to grind together, but not too finely. The salt will keep in an airtight container in a cool place for up to a month.

2. To make the Yuzu Miso Dressing, whisk all the ingredients together well in a bowl with 2 tablespoons of water. The dressing will keep in an airtight container in the refrigerator for up to a month.

3. Cut each 70g serving of beef into 'tataki blocks' about 5cm across x 3cm deep and as long as possible.

4. Place a cast-iron frying pan over the highest heat until smoking. Cover one side of the beef blocks with the Chilli Lime Salt and, adding the teaspoon of oil to the pan, sear the beef for about 10 seconds on each side until a good colour is achieved. Immediately transfer the seared beef to a plate and chill in the refrigerator to firm up ready for slicing. Once fully chilled, carefully cut into 3mm-thick slices and keep chilled until ready to serve.

5. To prepare the kale, pour the oil for deep-frying into a deep saucepan (at least 2 litres in capacity) and set over a medium-high heat. Make sure the kale is completely dry and then, when the oil reaches 180°C, deep-fry (one serving at a time) for about 10 seconds until crisp but still green in colour. Remove with a slotted spoon, drain thoroughly on kitchen paper and season with a little of the Chilli Lime Salt. Leave to cool to room temperature.

6. To serve, place the kale on a serving plate and top with the beef slices, then dress both with the Yuzu Miso Dressing. Add a small wedge of Pickled Daikon and a sprinkling of sesame seeds to each. Leave for 1 minute to come up to room temperature before serving.

Yaki Niku Beef Salad

We all love crisp noodles, so including them in a salad is a winner. This always goes down really well when we feature it on the menu.

Serves 4

Yaki Niku Marinated Beef

50g Barbecue Sauce (see page 65)

½ red chilli, sliced

250g picanha or other tender-cut beef, fat and sinew removed, cut into bite-sized slices 6mm thick

Yaki Niku Salad Dressing

100ml Mushroom Pickling Liquid (see page 29)

80ml rice wine vinegar

50ml Chilli Oil (see page 104)

15g caster sugar

5g Maldon sea salt

Salad

2 litres vegetable oil, for deep-frying

180g uncooked wavy Tokyo noodles

240g Yaki Niku Marinated Beef slices (see above)

1 cucumber, deseeded and sliced into 5mm julienne

4 Sliced Spring Onions (see page 118)

160g Pickled Shiitake, sliced 5mm thick (see page 29)

240ml Yaki Niku Salad Dressing (see left)

2 large handfuls of coriander, leaves picked

2 red chillies, sliced

1. To prepare the Yaki Niku Marinated Beef, combine the Barbecue Sauce and chilli in a bowl, then carefully fold in the beef. Cover and leave to marinate in the refrigerator for at least 1 hour.

2. To make the Yaki Niku Salad Dressing, mix all the ingredients together in a bowl.

3. Pour the oil into a deep saucepan (at least 4 litres in capacity) and set over a medium-high heat. When the oil reaches 180°C on a thermometer, carefully add the noodles, in 2 batches if necessary so as not to overcrowd the pan, and deep-fry for about 5 seconds until lightly golden and crisp. Remove with a slotted spoon and drain thoroughly on kitchen paper. Break the noodles into thirds.

4. Set a frying pan over a high heat. Add the drained beef slices and sear very quickly, just until well coloured on both sides. Remove from the pan immediately.

5. Mix the cucumber, Sliced Spring Onions, Pickled Shiitake and dressing together in a bowl.

6. To construct each serving, using your fingers, gently layer up the crispy noodles and dressed vegetables (reserving the dressing left in the bowl) as tall as you possibly can on a plate, using 3 layers of each.

7. Next, arrange the freshly seared beef, coriander leaves and sliced red chillies attractively on top and spoon the dressing from the bowl all over the top. Eat straight away so that the noodles haven't got time to go soggy.

Guinea Fowl & Avocado Salad

This is an incredible salad and an amazing dressing. You can replace the guinea fowl with roast chicken or fish.

Serves 2

Fried Guinea Fowl

200ml sake

20g fresh root ginger, peeled and roughly chopped

20g Maldon sea salt

1 tablespoon mirin

2 guinea fowl legs, thighs and drumsticks separated (use a sharp knife to cut through the knee joint)

2 litres rapeseed oil, for deep-frying

100g kara-age Flour (see page 60)

Salad

3 whole baby gem lettuces, trimmed, leaves separated and cut into bite-sized pieces

1 avocado, pitted, peeled and roughly chopped

40g Carrot Pickle (see page 33)

2 Sliced Spring Onions (see page 118)

12 pieces Cucumber Pickle (see page 35)

2 green chillies, sliced

80ml Barley Miso Lime Dressing (see page 18)

1 teaspoon toasted white sesame seeds, to serve

1. To prepare the Fried Guinea Fowl, blitz the sake, ginger, salt and mirin in a food processor until the ginger is finely chopped. Transfer to a bowl.

2. The guinea fowl thighs are normally large enough to cut into 2, creating 3 fairly equal pieces of thigh and drumstick per serving. Do this by cutting up against the bone on the side where the meat is thickest. (The 2 pieces with bones in should then be opened up a little to even out the cooking times. This is done by cutting down lengthways to the bone and slightly butterflying them open.) Mix the prepared guinea fowl with the blitzed sake mixture to coat, then cover and leave to marinate overnight, or for at least 3 hours, in the refrigerator.

3. Pour the oil into a large, deep saucepan (at least 4 litres in capacity) and set over a medium-high heat. Lift the guinea fowl portions straight from the marinade, shaking off the excess, and coat thoroughly with the Kara-age Flour. When the oil reaches 180°C on a thermometer, deep-fry the coated guinea fowl, turning once, for about 6 minutes until golden, crisp and cooked through. Remove with a slotted spoon and drain thoroughly on kitchen paper.

4. In a large bowl, using your fingers, gently mix all the salad ingredients, except the sesame seeds, together well, then divide between 2 serving plates. Top with the Fried Guinea Fowl and sesame seeds.

Fried Chicken Kara-age

Fried chicken is probably our favourite junk food and Japanese fried chicken is some of the best. We made this recipe a little different to some of the plainer versions available in Japan. It's incredibly popular in the restaurant.

Serves 12

**Kara-age Marinade
(makes 120ml)**

40ml sake

40ml soy sauce

40ml ginger juice, squeezed from finely grated fresh root ginger

**Kara-age Flour
(makes 240g)**

125g plain flour

80g rice flour

3½ teaspoons fine table salt

1½ teaspoons ground white pepper

½ teaspoon sansyo pepper

Fried Chicken Kara-age

4 litres rapeseed or other flavourless oil, for deep-frying

1.8kg boneless chicken thighs, cut into large bite-sized pieces

120ml Kara-age Marinade (see left)

240g Kara-age Flour (see left)

2 lemons, cut into 6 wedges each

1. To make the Kara-age Marinade, mix all the marinade ingredients together in a bowl.

2. To make the Kara-age Flour, mix all the flour ingredients together in a separate bowl.

3. Pour the oil into a deep saucepan (at least 4 litres in capacity) and set over a medium-high heat. Add the chicken to the marinade in a bowl and leave to marinate for a few seconds. Then remove, shaking off the excess marinade, and coat thoroughly in the flour mixture, dusting off the excess. When the oil reaches 180°C on a thermometer, deep-fry the chicken in batches so as not to overcrowd the pan, for about 6 minutes, until cooked through, golden and crispy. Remove with a slotted spoon, drain thoroughly on kitchen paper and serve with a lemon wedge on the side.

When deep-frying foods, for safety, use a pan that is at least twice as large as the volume of oil used.

Salmon Kara-age with Chilli Ponzu

Salmon is such a well-liked fish here in the UK. This dish works best with the fatty belly of the fish.

Serves 4

2 litres rapeseed or other flavourless oil, for deep-frying

400g salmon fillet, skin on

200ml Kara-age Marinade (see page 60)

200g Kara-age Flour (see page 60)

Maldon sea salt, crushed, to taste

4 lemon wedges

4 shiso leaves

160ml Orange Ponzu (see page 44)

Chilli Daikon

120g piece of daikon, peeled

1 red chilli, split lengthways but kept in one piece and deseeded

1. To make the Chilli Daikon, using a chopstick, drill a hole through the centre of the daikon. Slip the chilli on to the end of the chopstick, then insert in the hole and push the chilli through into the hole. Grate with an *oroshi* (Japanese daikon grater) or a fine grater. Squeeze any excess water from the grated chilli daikon. You should be left with a nice mix of grated daikon and chilli.

2. Pour the oil into a large, deep saucepan (at least 4 litres in capacity) and set over a medium-high heat. Using a sharp knife, cut the salmon across the grain into 1cm-thick slices. There should be a strip of skin at the bottom of each slice.

3. Add the salmon to the Kara-age Marinade and leave to marinate for 1 minute. Shake off the excess marinade and coat thoroughly in the Kara-age Flour. When the oil reaches 180°C on a thermometer, deep-fry, in 2 batches, for about 30 seconds (the ideal internal temperature for the salmon is 52°C). Carefully remove with a slotted spoon and drain on kitchen paper. Sprinkle with a little crushed Maldon sea salt and serve with a lemon wedge and a shiso leaf on the side, with the Orange Ponzu in a bowl and a small ball of the chilli daikon in a side dish.

Sweet Spicy Pig Bones with Barbecue Sauce

We use lots of pork bellies to make the chashu pork that is a topping to our ramen. Our bellies come to us from the butcher with the rib bones attached and we remove these before rolling the bellies. When we opened the restaurant, these bones were an easy win for the team's dinner but, a few weeks in, the team was sick of them... really sick of them. So we needed to come up with a dish using the bones that we could put on the menu and buy something else to feed the team. These pig bones evolved and our customers have been loving them ever since. We still give them to the team, but not too often...

Serves 2

1 rack pork belly ribs
(about 460g)

2 litres vegetable oil,
for deep-frying

160ml Barbecue Sauce
(see right)

30g Chilli Bits (see
page 129)

2 teaspoons toasted white
sesame seeds

1 Sliced Spring Onions
(see page 118)

**Barbecue Sauce
(makes 660ml)**

265ml soy sauce

25ml sesame oil

325g caster sugar

1 tablespoon kochujan
- MSG-free is best

6 garlic cloves, puréed
with a little of the soy
sauce

1. To make the Barbecue Sauce, combine the soy sauce, sesame oil and sugar in a saucepan and bring to the boil. Remove from the heat, then whisk in the kochujan and garlic purée. Keep warm for serving, or store in a sealed container in the refrigerator for up to a month.

2. To braise the ribs, slowly simmer the whole rack in a large saucepan of water for 1–1½ hours until the meat comes away easily from the bone. Chill completely in the cooking liquid. Once chilled, cut between each bone, making sure there is plenty of meat on each.

3. Pour the oil into a large, deep saucepan (at least 4 litres in capacity) and set over a medium-high heat. When the oil reaches 180°C on a thermometer, deep-fry the ribs, in batches, for 1–2 minutes until heated through. Remove and drain thoroughly on kitchen paper.

4. In a large bowl, mix the fried ribs with the warm sauce, Chilli Bits and sesame seeds until well coated. To serve, divide the ribs between 2 plates, spoon the remaining sauce on top and sprinkle with the Sliced Spring Onions.

Chashu Pork & Corn Croquettes

The ends of the chashu rolls don't look great on a bowl of ramen, so we chop them to make this instead. *Korokke*, as they are called in Japan, are of course foreign but are an example of how Japan's food has been influenced by Western traders.

Makes about 30

Pork and Corn Mixture
40g unsalted butter
½ medium white onion, cut into 4mm dice
1 tablespoon finely grated fresh root ginger
1 large garlic clove, finely grated
1 teaspoon shichimi togarashi
50g plain flour, seasoned with a pinch of fine table salt and ground white pepper, plus 4 tablespoons for coating

250ml milk
2½ tablespoons Soy Tare (see page 108)
50g Parmesan cheese, finely grated
600g Chashu Pork Belly or Neck trimmings (see page 123), most of the fat trimmed, cut into 1cm cubes
2 Roasted Sweetcorn cobs, kernals sliced off (see page 127), about 150g
4 Sliced Spring Onions (see page 118)

2 litres rapeseed or other flavourless oil, for deep-frying

Panko Breadcrumb Coating
25g toasted white sesame seeds
15g aonori (seaweed flakes)
250g panko breadcrumbs
6 eggs

To serve
Chilli Lime Salt (see page 54), to taste

1. For the Pork and Corn Mixture, melt the butter in a saucepan and sweat the onion over a low heat without colouring. Add the ginger, garlic and shichimi and cook for 1–2 minutes. Add the 50g seasoned flour and cook over a low heat, stirring frequently, for 10 minutes to cook out the floury taste. Mix the milk and Soy Tare together, then add little by little to the flour mixture, whisking to a smooth paste after each addition of liquid. Whisk in the Parmesan and then very gently fold in the Chashu Pork, Roasted Sweetcorn and Sliced Spring Onions. Cover the surface with cling film, leave to cool and then chill in the refrigerator for up to 24 hours, or until required.

2. For the Panko Breadcrumb Coating, mix the sesame seeds and aonori into the panko breadcrumbs and spread the mixture out in a shallow bowl. Crack the eggs into a second bowl, add a splash of water and beat together well. Put the 4 tablespoons of flour into a third bowl.

3. Divide the pork and corn mixture into 30g (heaped tablespoon) portions and then, using slightly wet hands,

shape each into a cylinder shape. Dip each croquette first into the flour, dusting off the excess, then into the egg mixture, turning to coat lightly, and finally into the panko breadcrumb mixture, turning to coat the surface lightly. Place, spaced out, on a tray.

4. The croquettes are deep-fried in 2 stages to ensure that the centre is hot and the outside is not too dark. Pour the oil into a large, deep saucepan (at least 4 litres in capacity) and set over a medium-high heat. When the oil reaches 150°C on a thermometer, deep-fry the croquettes, in batches, until they begin to turn pale golden. Carefully remove with a slotted spoon and drain thoroughly on kitchen paper. Increase the heat below the pan until the temperature of the oil reaches 180°C. Deep-fry the croquettes for a second time, again in batches, until golden brown and crisp all over. Remove and drain well as before. Serve hot, sprinkled with the Chilli Lime Salt.

Korean Fried Guinea Fowl

Nearly all birds fry well. But long before Korean fried chicken had become sought after in London, we had a supply of guinea fowl legs that were awesome, so we made this. Some recipes we develop for up to a year before we are happy, but this one was pretty much there first go. Now we serve the same sauce with wings in all our restaurants because people go mad for it.

Serves 8

8 legs of Fried Guinea Fowl (see page 59)

500g Korean Sauce (see right)

8 teaspoons toasted white sesame seeds

Korean Sauce (makes 500g)

150g kochujan

750ml Chilli Oil (see page 104)

75ml mirin

150ml rice wine vinegar

10 garlic cloves, roughly chopped

1. To make the Korean Sauce, put all the ingredients in a blender and blitz until smooth. The sauce will keep in an airtight container in the refrigerator for at least 2 weeks.

2. Warm the sauce through in a small saucepan, stirring frequently, for 10 minutes, but don't allow the mixture to boil.

3. In a bowl, mix the hot Fried Guinea Fowl with the warm sauce and sesame seeds until well coated, then serve.

Soft-shell Crab with Green Chilli Ginger Dressing

This dish has street food roots firmly in both South East Asia and also in the southern states of the US. But it also reflects the American influence of sushi in the West and the popular soft-shell crab roll. Soft-shell crabs have become a popular dish in Japanese restaurants around the world.

Serves 4

2 litres rapeseed oil, for deep-frying

4 soft-shell crabs, cleaned if live, or defrosted and drained slightly if frozen

100g potato flour

Green Chilli Ginger Dressing (makes about 150ml, enough for 4 generous servings)

50g drained canned or fresh jalapeño chillies

1 green chilli, deseeded

25g fresh root ginger, peeled and roughly chopped

½ teaspoon Maldon sea salt

½ teaspoon grapeseed oil

1 tablespoon soy sauce

1 teaspoon lemon juice

30ml (2 tablespoons) rice wine vinegar

1. To make the Green Chilli Ginger Dressing, add the jalapeños, green chilli, ginger, salt and grapeseed oil to a blender and blend until smooth.

2. Mix the soy sauce, lemon juice and vinegar together. With the blender running, gradually add the soy sauce mixture to the blended mixture, blending until well incorporated and smooth.

3. Pour the oil into a large, deep saucepan (at least 4 litres in capacity) and set over a medium-high heat. Coat the soft-shell crabs in the potato flour, shaking off the excess. When the oil reaches about 180°C on a thermometer, deep-fry the coated crabs for 4–5 minutes, depending on the size, until crisp. Remove with a slotted spoon and drain thoroughly on kitchen paper. Serve hot, with the dressing in bowls on the side for dipping.

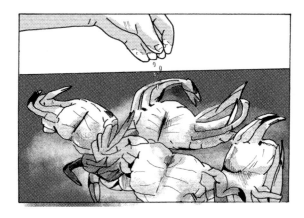

Padrón Peppers
with Sea Salt & Lemon

In Japan they use shishito peppers — a hybrid of the Padrón pepper from Spain and the jalapeño from Mexico — as a snack. This recipe offers something of that snacking spirit, and it's great to have in-house to use as a topping for our ramen.

Serves 2

4 tablespoons vegetable oil
100g Padrón peppers
Maldon sea salt
lemon wedges, to serve

1. Heat the oil in a small frying pan, add the Padrón peppers and fry for 10 seconds, turning frequently with tongs. Remove with a slotted spoon and drain on kitchen paper.

2. Mix with plenty of sea salt and serve with lemon wedges on the side.

Brussels Sprouts with Ponzu & Pomegranate

Yeah, sure, at Bone Daddies we serve a lot of meaty dishes, but we like to challenge ourselves to make vegetable dishes that are super-delicious too. This Brussels sprout dish will be a little unexpected for traditionalist Brussels sprout fans and is surely going to convert all those who think they don't like sprouts.

Serves 4

½ large pomegranate – choose a nice, dark red fruit
500g Brussels sprouts
2 litres rapeseed oil, for deep-frying

Maldon sea salt, crushed between the fingers, to taste
150ml Orange Ponzu (see page 44)
finely grated zest of ½ orange (without pith)

1. To prepare the pomegranate, hold the pomegranate, cut side down, over a bowl of water, gently hit the skin side with a wooden spoon and the seeds should easily pop out into the water. Continue until all the seeds have dropped out. Carefully pick the white bits out of the water and discard, then drain the seeds.

2. To prepare the Brussels sprouts, trim just a little from the base of each sprout, then cut halfway down into the head of the sprout. Rotate the sprout through 90° horizontally and cut all the way down through the head of the sprout. This will allow the layers in the head to open up during frying and result in a crispier sprout.

3. Pour the oil into a deep saucepan (at least 4 litres in capacity) and set over a medium-high heat. When the oil reaches 180°C on a thermometer, deep-fry the sprouts, in 2 batches, for 25 seconds. Remove with a slotted spoon and leave to cool for 2 minutes.

4. Reheat the oil and deep-fry the sprouts again for a further 25 seconds until golden and crisp. This second frying gives a crispier sprout without too much colouring. Drain thoroughly on kitchen paper.

5. Mix the sprouts thoroughly with a few pinches of sea salt in a bowl. Lay out on serving plates and top with the Orange Ponzu, pomegranate seeds and orange zest. Serve immediately.

Prawn & Squid Kaki-age

After tempura was introduced to Japan by the Portuguese, the kaki-age evolved. This is similar to a pakora in Indian cooking and you can put almost any veg into it. Serve it like this, or just with sea salt and lemon, to enjoy it in its purest form.

Batter (makes about 350g, enough for up to 7 servings of kaki-age)

1 egg

125g plain flour

Kaki-age (per serving)

2 litres vegetable oil, for deep-frying

20g squid, cleaned and cut lengthways into slices 5mm thick

20g raw tiger prawns, peeled, deveined and cut into 2cm pieces

15g sweet potato, peeled and sliced into 4mm julienne

15g carrot, peeled and sliced into 4mm julienne

15g parsnip, peeled and sliced into 4mm julienne

15g salsify, peeled and sliced into 4mm julienne (once prepared, keep in water with lemon juice added to prevent it turning brown)

5g red onion, sliced 4mm thick

pinch of chives, cut into 5cm lengths

50g Batter (see left), chilled

To serve (per serving)

2 tablespoons Orange Ponzu (see page 44)

1 lemon wedge

shichimi togarashi, to taste

1. To make the batter, beat the egg and 200ml ice-cold water together well in a bowl, then mix in the flour without overmixing – it is OK if a few small lumps remain. Cover and refrigerate until required.

2. For each serving of Kaki-age, pour the oil into a large, heavy-based saucepan (at least 4 litres in capacity), ideally very deep with a diameter of about 20cm to achieve the correct kaki-age shape with the minimum of fuss, and set over a medium-high heat. Carefully mix all the prepared seafood, vegetables and chives together thoroughly in a small mixing bowl. Add the chilled batter and toss to mix. When the oil reaches 170°C on a thermometer, slowly and carefully slide half the mixture into the hot oil, using a spatula to stop the mixture from spreading too much. You should be aiming for a 7cm-diameter disc of lightly battered seafood and vegetable mixture. Deep-fry for about 1–2 minutes on each side until lightly golden in colour and crisp and light – it will take a little practice to achieve the best results!

3. Remove with a slotted spoon, drain well on kitchen paper and sprinkle with salt. Repeat the process with the remaining mixture. Serve hot with Orange Ponzu, a lemon wedge and shichimi togarashi on the side.

Chicken & Prawn / Pork & Truffle Gyoza

During Ross's time as head chef of another Japanese restaurant, he visited Japan and ate a chicken *tsukune* (large grilled meatball) in a yakitori restaurant in Kyoto – it was incredible, the best he had ever had. We wanted to recreate this, but give it a twist, so we made one with prawn, chicken and chilli and wrapped it in caul fat. That dish was great, but we knew, as soon as we opened Bone Daddies, that we wanted to use the same recipe as a gyoza filling.

The Pork and Truffle Gyoza are quite simply two of our favourite things combined into one of our favourite things. Try them and have fun making them – the reward is definitely worth the effort.

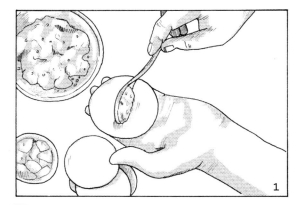

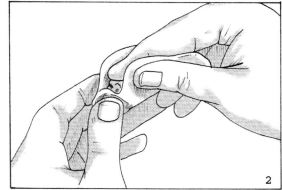

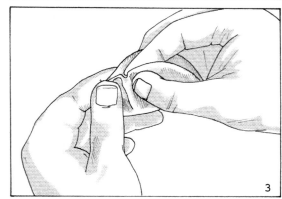

Chicken & Prawn Filling (makes 20 gyoza, enough for 4 servings)

200g minced chicken

100g peeled, deveined and finely chopped raw tiger prawns

2 tablespoons finely chopped onion

1 fresh chilli, finely chopped

1 teaspoon fine sea salt

2 teaspoons Chilli Oil (see page 104)

2 teaspoons sesame oil

1 teaspoon finely chopped fresh root ginger

1 garlic clove, finely chopped

freshly ground black pepper, to taste

30g water chestnuts, finely diced (optional)

Pork & Truffle Filling (makes 20 gyoza, enough for 4 servings)

250g minced pork

60g white cabbage, finely chopped

1 spring onion, finely chopped

20g truffle, finely chopped – if you can find sliced white truffles in oil, this works well, otherwise use white truffle oil

20g fine sea salt

To assemble each filling (makes enough for 4 servings)

20 gyoza skins

vegetable oil, for shallow-frying

To serve (enough for 4 servings)

120ml Orange Ponzu (see page 44)

1. Mix together all the ingredients for either (or both, separately) filling in a bowl, cover and chill in the refrigerator – this ensures that the mixture is easy to work with and not too soft. Adding the water chestnut to the Chicken and Prawn Filling will give it extra texture.

2. To assemble the gyoza, lay a gyoza skin in the palm of your hand and place a barely heaped teaspoon (15g) of the filling in the centre. Run a finger dampened with water around the outside edge of the skin, then fold each side up together and crimp along the edge to seal. The crimping can be as simple or fancy as you dare to attempt. Repeat with the remaining skins and filling.

3. To cook each batch of 20 gyoza, heat a little oil in a lidded nonstick frying pan over a medium-high heat. Add the gyoza, smooth side down, and cook until lightly coloured. Then add 75ml of water to the pan and quickly place the lid on to steam the gyoza. After 3–5 minutes, remove the lid and continue to cook until all the liquid has evaporated and the gyoza have a crispy golden base.

4. Serve immediately, with the Ponzu on the side.

In Japan, most ramen bars serve very few, if any, starters. We wanted to push beyond that, because the ramen scene in London was virgin.

FIRST

Gua Bao (Steamed Buns)

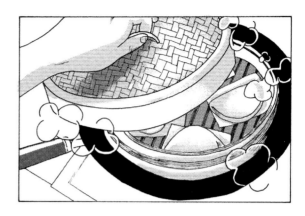

London has fallen in love with buns since we opened Flesh & Buns in August 2013 – only a few street food guys were around at that time. Because of limited space, we couldn't do any steam buns at a Bone Daddies until we opened our Kensington restaurant and decided to do four different buns there.

Makes 18 buns

15g fresh yeast or
7g sachet dried yeast or
3.5g (½ sachet) fast-action dried yeast
140ml lukewarm milk

35g caster sugar, or more if you prefer a sweeter flavour
500g plain flour (see tip, right), plus extra for dusting

1 teaspoon fine sea salt
1 tablespoon vegetable oil, plus extra for brushing

1. Mix the yeast, 145ml warm water, milk and sugar together in a bowl and leave to stand for 10 minutes.

2. Mix in the 500g flour to make a smooth, firm dough, then cover the bowl with cling film and leave in a warm place for at least 30 minutes until doubled in size.

3. Add the salt and oil to the dough and knead until well incorporated.

4. Place the dough on a floured surface and knead for 10 minutes until the gluten has been activated and the dough is smooth and elastic.

5. Cut the dough into 45g balls and give each a quick knead before rolling into a sphere. Then, with a rolling pin, roll each sphere into an oval shape about 3mm thick. Brush the dough with oil, then fold over in half and press together gently. Space out on a lightly oiled tray, cover with lightly oiled cling film and leave in a warm place to prove for 20 minutes until puffed and risen.

6. Carefully transfer to a warm bamboo steamer lined with greaseproof paper and leave to rest for 10 minutes. It is important that the steamer has a domed lid so that droplets of water don't drop on to the dough when cooking. Steam for 15 minutes.

7. You can reheat the buns when you are ready to eat – simply steam for 5–7 minutes; don't steam them for too long, otherwise they will turn yellow.

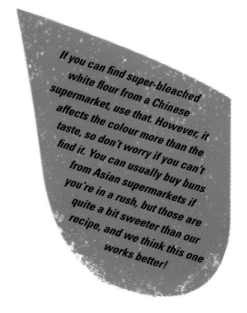

If you can find super-bleached white flour from a Chinese supermarket, use that. However, it affects the colour more than the taste, so don't worry if you can't find it. You can usually buy buns from Asian supermarkets if you're in a rush, but those are quite a bit sweeter than our recipe, and we think this one works better!

Bone Daddies was never trying
to re-create Japan exactly.

We wanted to create
our own style.

Boney D's Fried Chicken Bun with Kimchi Mayo, Cabbage & Pickled Cucumber

Our fried chicken is very popular, so we were sure we could make a bun that would go one better. It is like a dirty fried chicken sandwich on cheap white bread, but a bit more evolved…

Serves 1 (makes 2 buns)

2 Gua Bao (see page 82)

1½ tablespoons Kimchi Mayo (see right)

2 small pieces Chinese cabbage, leaves separated

40g Kimchi (see page 30)

25g Cucumber Pickle (see page 35)

110g Fried Chicken Kara-age (see page 60), thighs halved (rather than cut into pieces)

pinch of toasted white sesame seeds

Kimchi Mayo (makes 225g)

75g Korean Sauce (see page 68)

25g Kimchi Tare (see page 112)

125g Hellman's mayonnaise

1. First, make the Kimchi Mayo by mixing the ingredients together well in a bowl. This will keep in a sealed container in the refrigerator for up to 2 weeks.

2. Reheat the buns by steaming for 5–7 minutes until soft in the centre.

3. Open up the buns and spread with three-quarters of the Kimchi Mayo, then divide the cabbage leaves, Kimchi, Cucumber Pickle and Fried Chicken Kara-age between them. Finish with the sesame seeds and the remaining Kimchi Mayo.

4. Close the bun lids and skewer each with a bamboo teppo gushi.

Chashu Pork Bun with Sweet Chilli Soy Sauce, Pickled Cucumber, Spring Onion & Chilli

. . . .

Chashu Pork Buns have become a bit of a classic now and this is our take on it.

Serves 1 (makes 2 buns)

100g Chashu Pork Belly (see page 123), cut into 2 x 50g slices

3 tablespoons Sweet Spicy Soy Sauce (see page 24), without Chilli Bits

2 Gua Bao (see page 82)

15g Cucumber Pickle (see page 35)

½ red chilli, finely sliced

½ a Sliced Spring Onion (see page 118)

1. Preheat the oven to 200°C/Gas Mark 6. Combine the Chashu Pork Belly and the Sweet Spicy Soy Sauce (without Chilli Bits) in an ovenproof dish and heat through in the oven for 6–7 minutes.

2. Reheat the buns by steaming for 5–7 minutes until soft in the centre.

3. Open up the buns and divide the Cucumber Pickle, pork, chilli and Sliced Spring Onion between them, topping with plenty of the cooking sauce. Close the bun lids and skewer each with a bamboo teppo gushi.

Salmon Kara-age Bun with Chilli Ginger Mayo, Cabbage & Cucumber Pickle

In Asia, it wouldn't be customary to put fish in a bun, but we think of it as being like a posh fish finger sandwich. For this, it is best if you use the fatty salmon belly, but not essential.

Serves 1 (makes 2 buns)

2 Gua Bao (see page 82)

1½ tablespoons Green Chilli Mayo (see page 14)

30g Cucumber Pickle (see page 35)

100g Salmon Kara-age (see page 62), cut into 2 x 50g pieces

1 Sliced Spring Onion (see page 118)

½ green chilli, finely sliced

1. Reheat the buns by steaming for 5–7 minutes until soft in the centre.

2. Open up the buns and spread with three-quarters of the Green Chilli Mayo, then divide the Cucumber Pickle, Salmon Kara-age, Sliced Spring Onions and chilli between them. Finish with the remaining Green Chilli Mayo.

3. Close the bun lids and skewer each with a bamboo teppo gushi.

The History of Ramen

There's no one official story as to how ramen started and I've heard a few different versions. One is that, in the First World War, Japanese soldiers stationed in China learnt to cook a noodle-type dish called lamian and when they came back to Japan they started little street stalls cooking it. As these soldiers all returned to different parts of Japan they cooked lamian with what they had locally to them, which is how these different styles started.

So you have different styles, and accepted versions, of ramen created geographically, with a different noodle for example. There are so many different types of noodle: flat, round, thick, thin... Some are very dry and used as just a vehicle for the soup, while others use the soup as more of a sauce for the noodle. Down in the south they eat the noodles so dry, with such a low water content, that they're almost crunchy and raw tasting. They cook them for a very short time, in some places for only ten seconds. That crunch in a noodle - koshi in Japanese - is described as the 'backbone' of a noodle.

In Japan, people will typically talk about ramen in terms of the city it represents. So 'Tokyo ramen' is a light, chicken-based broth, with normally a wavy, bouncy noodle and quite simple toppings. On the other hand 'Hakata ramen' is from the south, which is famous for tonkotsu. Or 'Sapporo ramen', from the north of the country, is typically miso ramen.

A lot of these ramen variations depend on what people normally have locally to where they come from. This has then historically dictated the style. For example, tonkotsu pork broth (from the south) is very rich and can actually be pretty pungent and almost off-putting. When I went to the south I saw that not many people drank their soup; the noodles and toppings were eaten in the soup and then people would order kae-dama (another portion of noodles) and have the second portion in the leftover soup... and then in the end they would leave the soup. So while some people in Japan actually value the noodle over the soup, we've found that here in London people value the soup over the noodle, so people will drink the soup first of all and sometimes leave the noodles.

Ramen chefs
are the punks of
the food world
in Japan.

Tearing Up the Rule Book

Ramen has grown up out of many different influences. The Japanese food landscape is incredibly varied, but it essentially comes down to two categories: washoku and yoshoku. Washoku is traditional Japanese cuisine, things such as kaiseki ryori, traditional sushi, foods that have evolved or been invented in Japan. Yoshoku is foreign food that is now accepted as Japanese food culture: Japanese curry, for example. Curry was never historically part of the Japanese diet, but it has now become quintessentially Japanese in its sweet, mild form.

Ramen is a yoshoku and there are no rules. It's a stark contrast to other Japanese food cultures. For example, an edomae is a traditional edo-style sushi chef: nigiri only, no rolls. Edomae are so disciplined in how they work, everything is controlled and precise. As are kaiseki ryori chefs, who cook the traditional royal cuisine of Japan. Everything is very precise, very delicate - they almost make Michelin-star chefs in Europe look disorderly, they are just amazing.

Ramen chefs, on the other hand, they often work from little stalls and their environment has pots boiling everywhere so it is naturally more messy. They'll sometimes have towels or bandanas tied around their heads because it's so hot and sweaty, or Wellington boots on because they're slopping noodles around and splashing water onto the floor and there's shit going everywhere. They wear t-shirts but an edomae sushi chef wears a tie and a super-smart chef jacket. The two are night and day. I think ramen chefs are the punks of the food world in Japan. Because ramen is a yoshoku, it doesn't have the cultural, historical restrictions that washoku foods have, because the history isn't as deep rooted.

There's less opportunity to experiment with traditional Japanese food. If you go to a soba noodle restaurant anywhere in Japan, ultimately it's very similar. It's delicious, it's something to love and enjoy, but it's rooted by the history and culture surrounding soba. I don't think I would ever open a soba noodle restaurant. I would be scared to mess with that formula, because it's brilliant in its purest form.

Ramen's never had that history, so it's always been able to be whatever the chef wants it to be. I've always challenged people when they've said, 'oh that's not ramen' or, 'that's not right'. I say, 'well what do you mean that's not fucking right? Because tell me what's right!' Because in Japan there's no such thing as right when it comes to ramen, it just has to be balanced and delicious.

RAMEN

RAMEN BASICS

The following pages have all the recipes that you need to construct a great bowl of ramen. These are the basic components – broths, oils and fats, tares, noodles and toppings – that you can prepare in advance and have to hand to whip together a quick bowl for most of the ramen from page 136 onwards.

Broths

Pork Broth

Makes 4 litres

2 pigs' feet (about 500g), split in half – ask your butcher to do this

2kg pork shin bones (meat off), cut across the shank – ask your butcher to do this

400g pork back fat (skin and meat removed)

5cm-wide strip of pork skin from a pork belly

1 large white onion (about 200g), roughly chopped into 2cm pieces (if using a white-skinned onion, you don't need to peel it)

4 whole garlic cloves, peeled

1 green apple (about 150g), skin on, cored and roughly chopped into 2cm pieces

30g fresh root ginger, rinsed but not peeled and roughly chopped into 2cm pieces

1. Put the pigs' feet and pork shin in a large saucepan with about 1.5 litres of water, or enough to cover the bones by 2.5cm. Bring to the boil and continue boiling for 30 minutes, skimming any scum that rises to the surface and stirring throughout. Strain through a fine-mesh sieve into a very large saucepan or stock pot. Wash the bones thoroughly, discarding any brown or grey foam.

2. Top up the pork blanching broth with water to make about 7 litres. Return the pork bones with all the remaining ingredients and bring to a simmer, skimming frequently – the aim is to remove as much of the dark matter that surfaces as possible. Continue cooking, uncovered, over a medium-high heat for 15–20 hours, stirring and topping up the water regularly. The fat and skin will become soft and should be carefully removed, in batches, blitzed in a blender and then returned to the broth until you are left with a thick and creamy white broth.

3. Top up with water once more to the original level, stir well, then strain through a fine-mesh sieve, ensuring that any solids are pressed through to extract all their goodness. Cover and chill in the refrigerator for up to 3 days. Heat through when needed, or freeze for 4–6 months.

Making our pork broth

RAMEN

Mushroom Broth

Makes 2.4 litres

6 garlic cloves, peeled
and lightly charred with
a blowtorch

1 small piece green leek
top, well charred with
a blowtorch

3 sprigs of thyme

80g dried shiitake
mushrooms

2 medium onions (about
250g), well charred with
a blowtorch (see Tip)

50ml Soy Tare (see
page 108)

1. Tie the garlic, leek and thyme in a square of muslin into a bundle.

2. Put all ingredients into a large saucepan with 3 litres of water and bring to the boil. Turn off the heat, cover with cling film and leave to infuse in a cool place for at least 3 hours, but ideally overnight.

3. Strain the Mushroom Broth through a fine-mesh sieve, pressing the solids to extract as much flavour as possible. Discard the muslin bundle, but reserve the shiitake if you want to make the Mushroom Butter (see page 105) or Soy-braised Shiitake (see page 129).

4. The broth is now ready to use. Cover and chill in the refrigerator for up to 3 days and heat through when needed, or freeze for 4–6 months.

If you don't have a blowtorch, you can char the garlic, leek and onions in a smoking-hot griddle pan.

RAMEN

Chicken Broth

Makes 5 litres

1.5kg chicken wings

1.5kg chicken thighs (or any other chicken bones that you have)

10g konbu

10g dried shiitake mushrooms, rinsed and tied in a square of muslin into a bundle

25g fresh root ginger, rinsed but not peeled and cut into slices 1cm thick

100g green leek tops or green spring onion tops

1. To roast the chicken wings, preheat the oven to 200°C/Gas Mark 6 and spread the wings out on an oven tray. Roast for about 1 hour, turning the wings over halfway through, until golden and crisp.

2. Add all the chicken to a very large saucepan or stock pot and top up to the 4-litre mark with water, then add all the remaining ingredients. Bring to a simmer and continue simmering for 30 minutes, skimming any foam or solids which rise to the top. Skim off most of the chicken fat and reserve it for use in other recipes (see page 105).

3. Cover the pan with a tight-fitting lid and cook over a very low heat on the hob, or transfer to a lidded ovenproof pan and cook in the oven preheated to 150°C/Gas Mark 2, for 8–10 hours, checking every now and then. Skim once again, top up with water to make 5 litres, then drain the liquid into a large container. Once drained, press the solids and meat through a fine-mesh sieve, then mix the pressed broth with the drained broth, ensuring that it is evenly mixed.

4. Cover and chill in the refrigerator for up to 3 days and heat through when needed, or freeze for 4–6 months.

In the Bone Daddies Kitchen:
Making our chicken broth

Oils & Fats

. . . .

Chilli Oil

Makes 560ml

3 garlic cloves, peeled and finely diced into 5mm pieces

500ml oil, reserved from making Garlic Chips (see page 128), or vegetable or rapeseed oil

1 spring onion (about 25g), trimmed and finely sliced

10g fresh root ginger, peeled and finely diced into 5mm cubes

40g red chilli flakes

60ml (4 tablespoons) sesame oil

1. In a saucepan much larger than you need for the volume of ingredients, heat the garlic-flavoured or vegetable or rapeseed oil with the spring onion, garlic and ginger and cook over a medium heat until golden and crispy. Add the chilli flakes and sesame oil and mix well, then immediately turn off the heat. Continue mixing every few minutes until the oil is a strong red colour, but do not allow the chilli flakes to burn.

2. Leave to cool, then strain the oil into an airtight container, reserving the solids to make Chilli Bits (see page 129). Store the oil in a cool, dark cupboard for up to 2 months.

Mayu (Burnt Garlic Oil)

Makes 200ml

50g garlic cloves, peeled
200ml vegetable oil

1. Add the garlic to a blender and use a little of the oil to blend to a purée.

2. Transfer the garlic purée to a pan with the remaining oil and cook over a medium-low heat until seriously blackened. Reduce the heat to low and continue cooking until just black. Leave to cool.

3. Blend in a powerful blender until the mixture breaks down to form a smooth black oil. Store in an airtight container in a cool, dark cupboard for up to 2 months.

Negi Oil (Roast Spring Onion Oil)

Makes 500ml

1 trimmed spring onion
(50g when trimmed)
500ml vegetable oil

1. Cut the spring onion into 3mm dice.

2. Put into a pan with the oil and cook over a medium-low heat until just before they turn black. Leave to cool. Store in an airtight container in a cool, dark cupboard for up to 2 months.

Chicken Fat

Makes about 200g

fat skimmed from Chicken
Broth (see page 102)

1. Pass the fat skimmed from the top of the broth through a fine-mesh sieve. Cover and store in the refrigerator until needed.

Mushroom Butter

Makes 210g

140g braised shiitake
mushrooms reserved from
the Mushroom Broth (see
page 101)

70g unsalted butter, at
room temperature

1. Roughly chop the mushrooms into 1cm pieces. Cook in a dry frying pan until all the moisture has evaporated and they start to caramelize.

2. Add the mushrooms to the butter and blitz in a powerful blender until the mushrooms are reduced to 5mm pieces.

3. Remove the butter from the blender and roll into a 4–5cm-diameter cylinder. Wrap in cling film and tie at either end, then chill in the refrigerator until firm. Cut into 1cm-thick rounds and remove the cling film before using.

Chicken Fat

Chilli Oil

Mayu

Mushroom
Butter

Spicy Miso
Tare

IP Tare

Curry Tare

Kimchi Tare

Sesame Oil

Soy Tare

Negi Oil

Goma Tare

Shio Tare

Tares

· ·

Soy Tare

Makes 600ml

500ml soy sauce
20g caster sugar
90ml mirin

1. Add half the soy sauce and all the sugar to a saucepan and place over a low heat until the sugar has completely dissolved, but do not allow to boil. Add the remaining ingredients and stir to combine.

2. Store in an airtight container in a cool, dark cupboard for up to a month.

Shio Tare

Dashi (makes 1 litre)

15g konbu
30g bonito flakes

Makes about 1.3 litres

1 litre Dashi (see left)
100g Maldon sea salt
25ml mirin
2 teaspoons rice wine vinegar

25ml light soy sauce
100ml sake
100ml soy sauce

1. To make Dashi, soak the konbu in 1 litre of water in a bowl overnight.

2. Transfer to a saucepan, add the bonito flakes and cover the pan with clingfilm, then heat to almost boiling (95°C on a thermometer) and maintain for 1 hour, but don't allow to boil.

3. Strain the dashi mixture through a fine-mesh sieve into a bowl, add the salt, sake, mirin and vinegar and mix together thoroughly, then stir in both soy sauces and 50ml of water.

4. Store in an airtight container in a cool, dark cupboard for up to a month.

IP Tare

Makes 300ml

100ml Soy Tare (see page 108)

100ml Shio Tare (see page 108)

100ml soy sauce

1. Mix all the ingredients together until well combined. Store in an airtight container in a cool, dark cupboard for up to a month.

Spicy Miso Tare

Makes 430g

40g Chilli Bits (see page 129)

2 tablespoons mirin

1 garlic clove, peeled

1 green chilli, halved, deseeded (seeds reserved) and finely chopped

40g mugi (barley) miso

2 tablespoons soy sauce

1 tablespoon sesame oil

150g ryoriten shiro white miso

50g ishino saikyo miso

10g fresh root ginger, rinsed but not peeled, dried and finely chopped

1 spring onion, rinsed, dried and finely chopped

50ml Soy Tare (see page 108)

1 tablespoon akadashi (red) miso

1. Put the first 4 ingredients with the seeds from the green chilli (reserve the finely chopped chilli flesh) into a powerful blender and blitz to a fine paste. Empty into a large bowl.

2. Blitz the barley miso, soy sauce and oil together in the same blender until smooth, then add to the bowl.

3. Add all the remaining ingredients, including the green chilli, and mix together well to eliminate any lumps. This can be made up to 5 days ahead and kept in an airtight container in the refrigerator. Bring up to room temperature before using.

111 In the Bone Daddies Kitchen:
Making our kimchi tare

Goma Tare

Makes about 720g

1 spring onion (about 25g), finely chopped in 2mm slices

25g fresh root ginger, peeled and finely chopped in 2mm dice

70g caster sugar

100ml soy sauce

55ml Chilli Oil (see page 104)

360g goma (Japanese white sesame paste)

50g toasted white sesame seeds

50g toasted black sesame seeds

1. Add the spring onion and ginger to a powerful blender and blitz together well.

2. Add the remaining ingredients except the sesame seeds and blitz again.

3. Add the sesame seeds and stir until well combined. Cover and store in the refrigerator for up to 2 weeks.

Kimchi Tare (pictured left)

Makes about 200g

45g Kimchi (see page 30)

1 garlic clove

55ml soy sauce

50g kochujan

2 teaspoons Korean chilli powder

2 tablespoons Soy Tare (see page 108)

1½ teaspoons sesame oil

2 teaspoons mirin

1. Add the kimchi and garlic to a powerful blender and roughly blitz together.

2. Add the remaining ingredients and blitz together until you have a smooth paste.

3. Store in an airtight container in the refrigerator for up to 2 weeks.

Curry Tare

Makes 1.2 litres

50g unsalted butter

100g white onion, roughly chopped into 1cm pieces

20g fresh root ginger, roughly chopped into 5mm pieces

20g garlic (3 large cloves), roughly chopped into 5mm pieces

30g curry powder (S&B brand)

2 tablespoons plain flour

1 tablespoon garam masala

300ml Dashi (see page 108)

100g (1 small) peeled banana, chopped

100g (1 small) apple, cored and chopped

65g akadashi (red) miso

65g ryoriten shiro (white) miso

280ml Soy Tare (see page 108)

100g rice wine vinegar

30g Chilli Bits (see page 129)

1. Melt the butter in a saucepan and sweat the onion until translucent. Add the ginger and garlic and sweat again, then stir in the curry powder, flour and garam masala and cook, stirring, for 10 minutes over a medium-low heat. Gradually pour in the Dashi while stirring, stopping every now and then to stir the mixture thoroughly. Once incorporated, mix in the banana and apple.

2. Blend the cooked mixture with a stick blender until smooth. Add the both misos, Soy Tare, vinegar and Chilli Bits, and blend again with the stick blender. Store in an airtight container in the refrigerator for up to 2 weeks.

Noodles

The subject of Japanese noodles is almost infinitely vast, so the following is only a brief introduction to how we approach them at Bone Daddies.

A fundamental concept that is hard for people in the West to get their heads around is the fact that a bowl of ramen noodles should be eaten as fast as possible while being served as hot as possible. This is to ensure that the noodle is consumed in its optimum state – after 5 minutes or so, the noodles will have continued cooking and absorbed some of the soup, thereby losing their prized texture. The act of slurping the noodles as they enter your mouth is not only a sign of appreciation, but also serves to cool the noodles.

Japanese noodles are made using kansui, alkaline mineral salts such as sodium carbonate and potassium carbonate. These serve to strengthen the noodles and, after cooking, result in a firm, springy texture, as opposed to most Chinese-style noodles that are eaten with a soft texture throughout. It is this alkalinity that also gives Japanese noodles their yellow appearance, and not egg as most would expect.

Types of noodle

The two types of Japanese noodle we use and those featured in the recipes are straight tonkotsu and wavy Tokyo noodles.

Tonkotsu noodles are white in colour, slightly thinner than the Tokyo noodle and completely straight. Once cooked, the inner part of the noodle should remain firm – almost crunchy – and it is this firmness and texture that is one of the most important aspects of ramen and prized by the Japanese.

Tokyo wavy noodles are yellower in colour, a little thicker and, obviously, wavy. Once cooked, the noodle is much more springy to the bite and therefore a little softer but still with a good resistance when eating.

Buying noodles

Genuine fresh Japanese ramen noodles are currently not available on the high street in the UK. The best straight tonkotsu noodles you can buy are the simple dried or semi-dried Japanese ramen wheat noodles, which should contain only wheat flour, salt, mineral salts and water, but if correctly cooked they will still have a good, firm texture to the bite. The same applies to Tokyo wavy noodles, although some relatively decent fresh Japanese-style egg noodles can be found at Asian supermarkets.

Cooking noodles

We cook both types of noodle in exactly the same manner, in unsalted boiling water. Generally speaking, the thicker the noodle, the longer the cooking time required, so always boil according to the packet instructions, unless stated otherwise in the recipe.

Toppings

. . . .

Soy Bamboo

Makes about 220g

1 teaspoon sesame oil
200g drained canned sliced
bamboo shoots (or vacuum-
packed cooked bamboo
shoots sliced)
80ml soy sauce
2 teaspoons caster sugar
1-2 pinches of red chilli
flakes, to taste

1. Heat the sesame oil in a wok or frying pan and stir-fry the bamboo shoots until dry, then add the remaining ingredients with 1½ tablespoons of water and cook until dry.

Blanched Bean Sprouts

1. To prepare bean sprouts for using in ramen, blanch them in a saucepan of boiling water for 10 seconds, then drain.

Sliced Spring Onions

1. To prepare spring onions for our ramen, we slice them as finely as possible and rinse under running water for 30 minutes to remove the harshness. They are then left to drain in a wire sieve for at least 30 minutes.

2. If that sounds like too much effort, instead just make sure you soak your finely sliced onions in a bowl of iced water for at least 10 minutes, then drain before using.

Chashu Pork
Belly

Sliced Spring
Onions

Blanched
Bean
Sprouts

Nori Squares

Marinated
Eggs

Cock
Scratchings™

Soy Bamboo

Chilli Oil &
Chilli Bits

Marinated Eggs

Makes 4

4 large eggs
100ml soy sauce
2 teaspoons caster sugar

1. Using a thumb tack, pierce the egg before cooking. This gives a nice round shape and makes it easier to peel.

2. First, soft-boil the eggs by cooking them in a saucepan of simmering water for 6 minutes. Immediately drain and refresh under cold running water for 5 minutes, then shell.

3. Mix the soy sauce with 100ml of water and the sugar together in a bowl. Add the eggs and leave to marinate in the refrigerator for at least 3–4 hours, or overnight if possible.

Use a spoon to peel the egg after you crack it all over.

Nori Squares

1. These usually come in approximately 20cm squares. To prepare, fold in half lengthways and gently press the fold flat. Pull each side of the nori sheet gently and the halves will separate; each nori half sheet measures 20cm x 10cm. Repeat the folding process again and you end up with 4 quarter sheets of nori, each 10cm square.

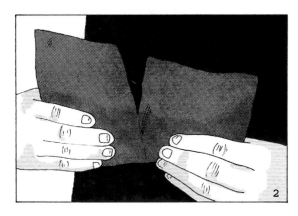

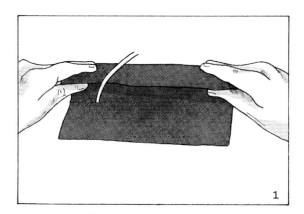

 123

Chashu Pork Neck

Makes about 700g, about 20 slices

1kg whole untrimmed pork neck, cut
lengthways in half and tied at regular
intervals with butcher's twine, but not
too tightly – ask your butcher to do this

Pork Braising Liquid (makes 1.5 litres)
750ml soy sauce
75g caster sugar

1. Preheat the oven to 180°C/Gas Mark 4.

2. Put all the ingredients for the Pork Braising Liquid in a
saucepan with 750ml of water and mix together well. Bring
just to the boil. This will keep for a couple of months in a
sealed container in a cool place,

3. Place the prepared pork necks in a deep ovenproof dish,
pour over the Pork Braising Liquid and cover with a tight-
fitting lid or foil. Braise in the oven for 1½ hours. Turn and
baste the pork with its cooking liquid, topping up with water
if necessary. Replace the lid or foil and roast for a further
1–1½ hours. The pork neck should be just starting to
fall apart.

4. Remove from the oven and leave to cool fully in the liquid.
Remove the cooled necks from the liquid and drain well.
Carefully remove the butcher's twine and wrap across the
length of the neck in cling film. Keep wrapped and whole in
the refrigerator and use slices as needed. This should keep
for up to 3 days.

Chashu Pork Belly

Makes about 700g, about 20 slices

1kg boneless, skinless pork belly,
rolled along its length and tied at
regular intervals with butcher's twine
– ask your butcher to do this
1.5 litres Pork Braising Liquid (see
left)

1. In a lidded saucepan large enough to contain the entire
piece of pork, simmer the rolled pork belly in the Pork
Braising Liquid, covered, for 2–2½ hours until the juices
run clear when a chopstick or a skewer is inserted into
the middle.

2. Turn off the heat and leave the pork to cool to room
temperature in the liquid. Then lift out the pork on to a
chopping board and carefully remove the butcher's twine.

3. Wrap tightly with cling film in the same direction as the roll
– this will help hold the roll in place while chilling and slicing.

4. Chill in the refrigerator overnight. Keep wrapped and
whole in the refrigerator and use slices as needed (3mm-
thick slices for most ramen toppings). This should keep for
up to 3 days.

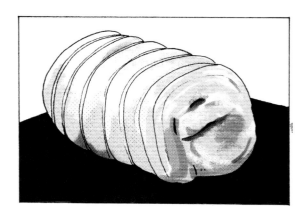

RAMEN

The ultimate point
of ramen is just that
it has to be delicious.

Cock Scratchings™ (pictured on page 124)

Makes 200g

1.5kg raw chicken skin
(some can be reserved from
the chicken thighs used
for Pulled Chicken, see
page 164)
2 teaspoons shichimi
togarashi

pinch of aonori (seaweed
flakes)
pinch of caster sugar
large pinch of fine table
salt

1. Preheat the oven to 190°C/Gas Mark 5.

2. Check the raw chicken skin for any remaining feathers, carefully removing any using a blowtorch or over a gas flame. Roast on an oven tray for 20 minutes, turning frequently to ensure that it cooks evenly. Drain off the fat and return the skin to the oven for 5–10 minutes to finish cooking – it should be deep golden and crispy, with no soft parts. Drain once again. Reduce the oven temperature to 120°C/Gas Mark ½.

3. Carefully crush the roasted chicken skin into evenly sized pieces about 5mm. Line the oven tray with plenty of kitchen paper, place the roasted chicken skin pieces on top and return to the oven for 20–25 minutes. The paper should now be saturated with the excess fat, while the Cock Scratchings™ are free from oil. Leave to cool. Mix thoroughly with the remaining ingredients.

Ask your butcher to keep some chicken skin for you to make this recipe – it shrinks down a lot!

Roasted Sweetcorn

Makes about 16-20 strips

2 sweetcorn cobs, husks
removed

1. Cook the sweetcorn cobs in a large saucepan of boiling water for 10 minutes, then drain and refresh under cold running water. Pat dry with kitchen paper.

2. Lightly char the cobs on all sides over a gas burner set to a high heat.

3. Standing each cob in turn upright on its base, carefully slice down its length just deep enough to reach the core, turning the cob 4–5 times, giving you nice strips of roasted corn.

Garlic Chips

Makes about 60g

100g peeled garlic cloves
500ml cold milk
2 litres rapeseed oil, for
deep-frying

1. Using a mandoline with a hand guard, lay a garlic clove on its side and slice lengthways from root to tip 2mm thick. Repeat with the remaining garlic cloves. As you are slicing, keep checking that the thickness remains the same throughout. This is necessary to result in good garlic chips, as they will then cook evenly. Don't try to slice the garlic cloves all the way to the very end – reserve the trimmings if you like to use in the Chilli Oil and Chilli Bits recipes (see pages 104 and 129).

2. Put the garlic slices and milk into a saucepan and slowly bring to a simmer, stirring frequently. Simmer for 15 minutes until the garlic is just soft and has lost most of its harshness.

3. Strain off the milk, then rinse the garlic under cold running water to remove all traces of milk and cool down. Strain again and dry the garlic chips between a few layers of clean kitchen towel – pressing gently to help make sure they are thoroughly dry.

4. Heat the oil in a large saucepan (at least 4 litres in capacity) over a medium-high heat to 150°C. Carefully add half the blanched garlic to the hot oil. Allow the initial steam to fry off, then start to slowly mix with a wooden spoon. As you stir continuously, the oil temperature should initially be reduced to no lower than 110°C, then slowly start to increase to 140°C. Once this temperature is reached, reduce the heat and stir until the garlic is evenly coloured and a very pale golden colour. Using a sieve, lift the garlic chips out and drain on kitchen paper. Once cooled, they should be crisp and ready to use. Reserve the leftover oil and use to add an extra level of flavour to the Chilli Oil recipe (see page 104). The Garlic Chips will keep in a sealed container in a cool, dark place for up to a week.

Soy-braised Shiitake

Makes about 180g

125g braised dried
shiitake mushrooms,
reserved from making
the Mushroom Broth (see
page 101)

Soy Braising Liquid
4 teaspoons Soy Tare (see
page 108)
2 teaspoons mirin

1. Mix all the ingredients for the Soy Braising Liquid together in a saucepan with 3 tablespoons of water, add the shiitake and simmer gently, stirring frequently, until only a little liquid remains but the mushrooms are still moist. Cool quickly, stirring.

2. Once cooled, the shiitake can be cut into 6mm-thick slices and are ready to use.

Chilli Bits

Makes about 80g

80g solids reserved from
making Chilli Oil (see
page 104)
½ teaspoon caster sugar
Chilli Oil (see page 104),
for covering

1. Blitz the first 2 ingredients in a small food processor until everything is an even, chunky size.

2. Transfer to a bowl and add enough Chilli Oil to cover. Keep covered in a cool place for up to 2 months.

Eggs at
9 o'clock

Making & Eating Ramen

Although there are no rules, the basic premise of ramen is that there are five components. First into the bowl is the tare, the seasoning for the soup, which goes in with the fat (the second component). Then (third) the broth goes on top of that and it's all mixed together. Then you put the noodle into that (four) and then the various toppings, which can be vegetables, braised meats, or pickled veg such as bamboo (component five), and possibly finish with some more fat on top of that. Having said that, we do have a fairly precise set-up for our bowls in the restaurant – eggs are always placed at 9 o'clock in front of the customer.

When we opened, we upset Japanese people because our kitchen is below our dining room and we were struggling to keep the bowl hot enough by the time it got to them. So we changed a lot of things to try to keep it hot. Many Japanese people are used to sitting at a ten-seat ramen counter where often the chef will pass you a bowl of ramen as soon as he's finished making it. And that's because, to get the most out of your ramen and to really enjoy the flavours, it's important to eat it fast, while it's very hot. There are really busy ramen bars in train stations that don't even have seats – you stand up to eat your bowl of ramen. I've timed people there that have been given a bowl and easily finished it inside ten minutes. And it's boiling hot, like fucking kill-your-mouth hot! But they'll do it in ten, because it's down to technique. In New York I've timed the average westerner eating a bowl of ramen in thirty-five minutes. In London people take forty-five minutes, fifty minutes. In London and New York you see people stopping to take a photo first, which is the worst thing you can do to a bowl of noodles because as soon as the noodle is in the soup it's already changing, absorbing soup and getting soggier.

I've joked that we should put timers on the table to advise customers to complete their bowl of ramen quickly, to really appreciate all of the effort that goes into making a really great bowl. I guess in London going out for ramen is more of a social exercise. Although we are getting more people in Bone Daddies who come in solo just to have a bowl of ramen and leave, which is great because we know they're appreciating the value of it, not just talking shit and letting it destroy itself. Obviously people can do what they want and we are very glad they like what we do, we just want them to have an amazing bowl at its best.

The follow-on to the eating quickly idea is that you need to make a nice slurping sound. Slurping loudly is a sign of appreciation that what you're eating is delicious. So technically, in a ramen bar, the only sounds you should hear are the slurping of happy customers, but at Bone Daddies rock'n'roll is an important element of the brand, and that came as a surprise to a few Japanese customers. But we never set Bone Daddies up to recreate Japan, we set it up to cater for Londoners: it's our interpretation of ramen, the way we want to deliver it, for a London audience. Having said that, people from the Shin-yokohama Raumen Museum in Japan visited a few years ago to document the ramen boom in Europe. They liked all of our ramen and we chatted about how the ultimate point of ramen is just that it has to be delicious. There are no rules beyond that. They tried all the ramen in London and we are the only place to feature on their global ramen map.

THE RAMEN

Ramen-making Tips

* Make sure you have all the ingredients laid out before starting to make a bowl so that you can work quickly.

* Have one pot ready with hot broth and another with boiling water for cooking the noodles.

* All noodles used in ramen soups should be firm when cooked. This doesn't always apply to ramen salads, dipping ramen and mazemen, however, where the degree of cooking is specified in the individual recipes.

* All tares should go into the serving bowl at room temperature, not straight from the refrigerator.

* We usually use the Fancy grade of Kikkoman soy sauce.

* Katsuo bushi (bonito flakes) should always be blitzed to a powder before using in recipes (with the exception of dashi, see page 108).

* All hot ramen should be served in a hot serving bowl; all cold ramen should be served in a cold serving bowl.

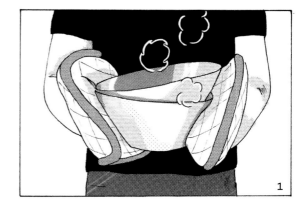

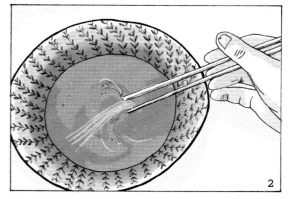

Tonkotsu Ramen

Hakata on Kyushu island is the town famous for tonkotsu, but this thick, rich pork broth is popular throughout the whole region, each place making it with small differences. For example, the Kumamoto style of making tonkotsu in some ways is a better reflection than the Hakata style of what we do, with the garlic chips that we add. Tonkotsu ramen is by far the most represented style here in London and has only in the last ten years become popular in Tokyo. Having eaten many bowls in Japan in the name of research, from *yatai* stalls to the very original *Ippudo*, we noticed that the locals do not very often seem to finish the broth. It is almost as if they value the thin, straight, almost raw noodles more than the broth and use the broth more as a 'sauce'. Because a lot of effort goes into making the broth, one restaurant was very excited to thank us for finishing ours and even had the *kanji* symbol for thanks printed on the bottom of the bowl for those who got that far. Some of our bowls have 'thanks' written into the bottom of them for the same reason.

We do a few things intentionally differently when making tonkotsu: we don't use *beni-shoga*, the red pickled ginger often served in Japan, because of the food colouring in it. Instead, we use a naturally coloured, great-quality sushi ginger and we add garlic chips. It takes a huge amount of time and effort to make this soup well and there is no single traditional recipe, so improvise with what we have done here and come up with your own house broth. Ultimately, it just has to be delicious.

A quick note about the Mayu: continually, while learning to cook Japanese food, we have encountered so many things that go against what you get taught by European chefs – and this is one thing that would blow most people's minds – the garlic is burnt. This is a big no-no normally, but run with it, as it becomes tasty on most soups.

Makes 1 serving

2 tablespoons Shio Tare (see page 108)

300ml hot Pork Broth (see page 97)

100g straight white tonkotsu noodles, cooked (see page 117)

30g Blanched Bean Sprouts (see page 118)

2 x 25g slices Chashu Pork Belly (see page 123)

1 Sliced Spring Onion (see page 118)

20g Soy Bamboo (see page 118)

2 Marinated Eggs (see page 120), halved

1 tablespoon Mayu (see page 104)

1 teaspoon sushi ginger, squeezed and well drained, then cut into 2mm shreds

1 scant teaspoon Garlic Chips (see page 128)

1. Put the tare and broth into a hot serving bowl and mix together well. Add the rest of the ingredients in the order above and serve immediately.

IP Tonkotsu Ramen

· ·

Our tonkotsu is our most popular ramen. When we heard that the Japanese ramen chain, Ippudo, was opening in London, Ross challenged Tom to make a Bone Daddies' version of the famous red spice on their ramen. Ours turned into more of a sauce and we put it on the menu before Ippudo opened, calling it IP, an abbreviation standing for both 'Ippudo' and 'intellectual property'. We were having fun but taking the piss also. A year later we made a pork cheek chashu and panko fried it – it was bloody tasty on the IP Tonkotsu, so the Cheeky IP was born (see page 140). We kept more of a traditional topping alongside this version, with the wood ear mushrooms.

IP Sauce with Chashu (makes about 290g, enough for 4 generous servings)
1 small garlic clove, roughly chopped
1 tablespoon Chilli Bits (see page 129)
25g Kimchi trimmings (see page 30)
2 teaspoons Korean chilli power
2 teaspoons sesame oil
25g Ryoriten shiro (white) miso
45g mugi (barley) miso

25ml Soy Tare (see page 108)
½ teaspoon bonito powder (see page 132)
½ red chilli, chopped
70g Chashu Pork Belly (see page 123), chopped

Ramen (per serving}
20g dried wood ear mushrooms
2 tablespoons IP Tare (see page 109)
300ml hot Pork Broth (see page 97)

100g straight white tonkotsu noodles, cooked (see page 117)
1 Sliced Spring Onion (see page 118)
2 x 25g slices Chashu Pork Belly (see page 123)
60g IP Sauce with Chashu (see left)
2 tablespoons Mayu (see page 104)

1. To make the IP Sauce with Chashu, blitz all the ingredients (except the Chashu Pork Belly) with 90ml of water to a fine paste in a small food processor or blender, stopping the machine to stir the ingredients every now and then so that they blend evenly. Mix in the chopped pork to finish.

2. Put the dried wood ear mushrooms in a bowl and cover with just-boiled water from the kettle. Leave to rehydrate for 20 minutes, then drain well. Cut into 3mm slices.

3. To construct the ramen, put the tare and broth into a hot serving bowl and mix together well. Add the rest of the ingredients in the order above, adding the rehydrated mushrooms after the Sliced Spring Onion and before the pork. Serve immediately.

Cheeky IP Tonkotsu Ramen

Follow the recipe for the IP Tonkotsu Ramen on page 138, but substitute the Crispy Braised Pork Cheeks (see below) for the Chashu Pork Belly. These are served on the side to keep them crispy and can then be dipped into the ramen as and when you feel like it!

Crispy Braised Pork Cheeks

Makes enough for 4 servings

4 large pork cheeks
600ml Pork Braising Liquid (see page 123)
2 tablespoons plain flour

1 egg, lightly beaten with 1 tablespoon water
90g panko breadcrumbs
2 litres rapeseed oil, for deep-frying

1. Place the pork cheeks and Pork Braising Liquid into a saucepan over a medium heat and gently boil for 1½–2 hours – you will know they are ready when you can easily bite through one of the cheeks and the connective tissue inside has turned to jelly. Leave the cheeks to cool in the braising liquid before removing them and patting dry with kitchen paper.

2. Cut each braised cheek into large, bite-sized pieces (about 3 per cheek). Have 3 shallow bowls ready. Put the plain flour in the first, the beaten egg mixture in the second and the panko in the third. Working in batches, dip the cheek pieces in the flour first, tossing to coat and shaking off the excess, then into the egg mixture until lightly coated. Lastly, toss each cheek piece in the panko breadcrumbs to coat. You can repeat the coating process for extra-crisp cheeks, in which case you will need to double up on the egg and panko quantities.

3. Pour the oil into a deep saucepan (at least 4 litres in capacity) and set over a medium-high heat. When the oil reaches 180°C on a thermometer, deep-fry the coated cheek pieces, in 2–3 batches, until golden brown all over, turning them frequently so that they colour evenly. Remove with a slotted spoon and drain thoroughly on kitchen paper. Serve straight away.

Niboshi Tonkotsu Ramen

We have started to mess with our broths and tares over the last year or so, just to add other elements. In the tare here the *niboshi* and *bonito* add a real fishiness to the pork – it gets richer and a bit smelly, but in a super-good way.

Fried Niboshi (makes 4 servings)

500ml rapeseed oil, for deep-frying

20 whole niboshi (dried baby sardines)

Ramen (per serving)

2 tablespoons IP Tare (see page 109)

1 tablespoon bonito powder (see page 132)

1 tablespoon chopped Chinese chives (gau choi)

300ml hot Pork Broth (see page 97)

100g Tokyo wavy noodles, cooked (see page 117)

30g Blanched Bean Sprouts (see page 118)

20g Soy Bamboo (see page 118)

2 x 25g slices Chashu Pork Belly (see page 123)

2 Nori Squares (see page 120)

1 teaspoon bonito powder (see page 132)

5 Fried Niboshi (see left)

1. To prepare the fried niboshi, pour the oil into a deep saucepan (at least 1 litre in capacity) and set over a medium-high heat. When the oil reaches 180°C on a thermometer, deep-fry the niboshi for 10 seconds, then remove with a slotted spoon and drain thoroughly on kitchen paper.

2. To construct the ramen, put the tare, bonito powder, Chinese chives and broth into a hot serving bowl and mix together well. Add the rest of the ingredients in the order above and serve immediately.

KimTonPam

Cheese in ramen has been popping up for years now in Japan, but it's a funny one here in London, because it's not 'traditional'. This one is a bit of an evolved tare. Very tasty, it has become a firm favourite.

Makes 1 serving

2 tablespoons Kimchi Tare (see page 112)

1 tablespoon Shio Tare (see page 108)

300ml hot Pork Broth (see page 97)

100g straight white tonkotsu noodles, cooked (see page 117)

20g Soy Bamboo (see page 118)

50g Pulled Chicken (see page 164)

45g Kimchi (see page 30)

1 strip Roasted Sweetcorn (see page 127)

1 Marinated Egg (see page 120), halved

1 Sliced Spring Onion (see page 118)

2 tablespoons Mayu (see page 104)

20g Parmesan cheese, finely grated

1. Put the tares and broth into a hot serving bowl and mix together well. Add the rest of the ingredients in the order above and serve immediately.

Pig Pig Pig Ramen

The original idea for this was 'let's use at least three different bits of pig' – like a celebration of our favourite animal, but focusing on the fun bits. This is head cheese chashu-style: a lot of prep up front, but a simple bowl after that.

Pigs' Ear Terrine (makes 20 slices)

1kg (about 8) pigs' ears – ask your butcher

1.5 litres Pork Braising Liquid (see page 123)

Pig's Head Terrine (makes about 22 slices)

1 pig's head – ask your butcher

4 litres Pork Braising Liquid (see page 123)

Ramen (per serving)

2 tablespoons Shio Tare (see page 108)

300ml hot Pork Broth (see page 97)

100g straight white tonkotsu noodles, cooked (see page 117)

30g Blanched Bean Sprouts (see page 118)

50g Chashu Pork Belly (see page 123), sliced

1 Sliced Spring Onion (see page 118)

20g Soy Bamboo (see page 118)

1 Marinated Egg (see page 120), halved

2 slices Pig's Head Terrine (see left)

2 slices Pigs' Ear Terrine (see left)

3 Crispy Braised Pork Cheeks (see page 140, but here we prefer just to braise the cheeks, omitting the deep-frying in breadcrumbs stage)

½ tablespoon Mayu (see page 104)

1 teaspoon sushi ginger, squeezed and well drained, then cut into shreds 2mm thick

1 scant teaspoon Garlic Chips (see page 128)

Continued

RAMEN

Pig Pig Pig Ramen (continued)

1. To make the Pigs' Ear Terrine, wash the ears thoroughly and singe off any hairs with a blowtorch or over a gas flame.

2. Place the pigs' ears and Pork Braising Liquid in a large saucepan and simmer for 3–4 hours until they are soft but the cartilage is still resistant to the knife. Remove from the heat and leave to cool to room temperature.

3. Line a terrine dish or mould or loaf tin, about 20cm x 10cm, with cling film, leaving enough overhanging to fold over and cover the top. Layer each ear carefully into the terrine dish, pressing down as you go. Pour over just enough of the cooking liquid to fill the gaps and cover the ears. Fold the excess cling film over the top to seal and tap the dish against the work surface to allow any air bubbles to escape. Find a piece of heavy-duty card or wood that just fits inside the dish and press down evenly, weighting it down with a few heavy food cans. Chill in the refrigerator overnight.

4. Remove the dish and cling film, and slice as required to serve.

5. To make the Pig's Head Terrine, wash the pig's head thoroughly and singe off any hairs as for the pigs' ears. In a huge pan (at least 12 litres in capacity), simmer the head in the Pork Braising Liquid for about 3 hours until the meat comes away easily from the bone. Remove from the heat and leave to cool to room temperature in the liquid. Remove the head onto a work surface fully lined with cling film, leaving the braising liquid in the pan. Trying your best not to break the skin, carefully peel the meat, fat and skin away from the bone, laying it out skin side down on the cling film. Don't worry if the skin does break, however, as you can simply patch it together before rolling.

6. Pick the remaining meat from the head and jaw into a large mixing bowl. Be sure to check all the nooks and crannies, where a lot of meat tends to be hiding. Discard all the bones and also any bits that are hard and don't look like meat, skin or fat, such as the insides of the eyes, the hard nose cartilage and the roof of the mouth. There won't be very much wastage.

7. Remove any large pieces of fat and set aside. Any large pieces of meat should be broken down into smaller pieces before adding to the bowl.

8. For the adventurous, using a large knife, split the skull in half and scoop out the brains, adding it to the bowl.

9. Give the meat in the bowl a gentle mix, and it's at this point that you need to decide if there is enough fat in the mixture to hold everything together. If not, break in a few more pieces of the reserved fat until you have a higher ratio of fat to meat.

10. You should now have laid out on the cling-filmed surface the relatively clean pig's head skin. Spread the meat mixture over the skin and then, using the cling film underneath, roll the skin up and over the meat mixture to form a long sausage shape, about 40cm in length and as thick as you want, twisting the cling film at either end to secure the rolled terrine.

11. Roll the terrine in 3 more layers of fresh cling film, then chill in the refrigerator overnight. You can then slice the terrine as you desire to serve – keeping the cling film in place makes this a little easier.

12. To construct the ramen, put the tare and broth into a hot serving bowl and mix together well. Add the rest of the ingredients in the order listed and serve immediately.

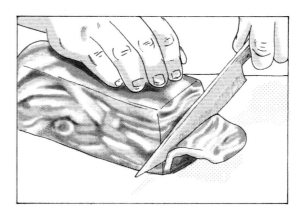

We want to push
the world of ramen
outside of Japan.

Crab Tonkotsu

We set Elia, one of our chefs, the goal of making a brown crab meat tare. It was quite a journey, but the team eventually got it there. It really challenges the idea of what a bowl can be, but is still really simple. The kale on this works very well; it was the first time we used kale, but we will be doing much more with it in the future.

Crab Tare (makes 4 servings)

60ml (4 tablespoons) Chilli Oil (see page 104)

150g brown crab meat

100ml IP Tare (see page 109)

½ tablespoon bonito powder (see page 132)

1 large garlic clove, peeled

Soft-shell crab (makes 4 servings)

2 whole soft-shell crab, cleaned if live, or defrosted if frozen, halved

1 tablespoon potato flour

4 litres rapeseed oil, for deep-frying

Ramen (per serving)

1 medium curly kale leaf, tough stalk removed

25g slice of Chashu Pork Belly (see page 123)

100g Crab Tare (see left)

210ml hot Pork Broth (see page 97)

70ml Dashi (see page 108), heated through

100g Tokyo wavy noodles, cooked (see page 117)

30g Blanched Bean Sprouts (see page 118)

½ deep-fried soft-shell crab (see left)

1 small spring onion, in 1cm slices (washed but not soaked)

2 tablespoons Chilli Oil (see page 104)

pinch of toasted black sesame seeds

Continued

Crab Tonkotsu (continued)

1. To make the Crab Tare, blitz all the ingredients together in a small food processor, then pass through a fine-mesh sieve to ensure that there are no fragments of crab cartilage or shell.

2. Blanch the kale (remember to use enough for the number of ramen servings you are making) in plenty of boiling water for about 5 seconds. Drain and refresh under cold running water. Drain thoroughly and set aside.

3. Quickly colour the Chashu Pork Belly in a hot griddle pan or under a hot grill. Keep warm.

4. Dust the crab half with the potato flour, shaking off the excess.

5. Pour the oil into a deep saucepan (at least 2 litres in capacity) and set over a medium-high heat. When the oil reaches 180°C on a thermometer, deep-fry the crab half for 2–3 minutes, turning frequently, until cooked through. Remove with a slotted spoon and drain thoroughly on kitchen paper.

6. To construct the ramen, add the tare and hot broth to each hot serving bowl and mix together well. Add the rest of the ingredients to the bowl in the order listed, adding the blanched kale, browned pork belly and fried crab after the Blanched Bean Sprouts and before the spring onion and sesame seeds.

To really get the
most value from
a bowl of ramen,
eat it as quickly
as possible.
Then talk.

RAMEN

That crunch
in a noodle
– koshi in Japanese –
is the 'backbone'
of the noodle.

Niboshi Ramen or Tsukemen with Black Pepper Vinegar

. . . .

This takes a new look at the relationship of dried fish in a tare and serving it *tsukemen*-style. It's strong and rich and we explored the use of fried chashu as a topping for the first time here…a lot more will definitely follow.

Niboshi Tare (makes about 250g, enough for 4 servings)

45g niboshi (dried baby sardines), blitzed to a powder

25g katsuo bushi (bonito flakes), blitzed to a powder (see page 132)

15g fresh root ginger, peeled and finely diced

2 spring onions, roughly chopped

40g garlic cloves, peeled and roughly chopped

100ml Negi Oil (see page 105)

300g Soy Tare (see page 108)

Black Pepper Vinegar (makes about 190ml, enough for 4-6 servings)

1 tablespoon freshly ground black pepper

175ml rice wine vinegar

Ramen (per serving)

1 tablespoon vegetable oil

80g Chashu Pork Belly (see page 123), cut into 2cm cubes

60g Niboshi Tare (see left)

300ml hot Pork Broth (see page 97)

100g Tokyo wavy noodles, cooked (see page 117, if making Tsukemen, cook for twice as long and blanch in cold water before serving on the side of the soup)

1 whole Marinated Egg (see page 120)

very small handful (about 10g) curly kale, tough stalks removed, blanched in boiling water for 10 seconds and drained

5 spring onions, 7.5cm long, blanched in boiling water for 20 seconds and drained

1 teaspoon niboshi powder (remove niboshi head and stomach contents and blitz to a fine powder)

1. To make the Niboshi Tare, blitz all the ingredients together in a blender to a paste. It should be as smooth as possible, so stop the machine regularly and redistribute the ingredients before blending again.

2. To make the Black Pepper Vinegar, stir the pepper into the vinegar in a small saucepan and bring to the boil. Remove from the heat and leave to cool. This will keep in a sealed container in a cool, dark place for up to 2 months.

3. Heat the vegetable oil in a frying pan or wok set over a medium-high heat, add the Chashu Pork Belly cubes and fry until browned on all sides.

4. Whisk the tare with the hot Pork Broth in each hot serving bowl, then construct the ramen in the order above (reserve the noodles to the side if serving as a tsukemen (dipping ramen), adding the fried pork cubes after the noodles and before the Marinated Egg.

5. The dish can be served either as a bowl of ramen or as a tsukemen. Either way, serve with the Black Pepper Vinegar on the side for everyone to add to taste.

Yuzu koshō Tonkotsu

A classic soba and udon noodle condiment, adding yuzu kosho into a tare just pushes this tonkotsu into another direction – fresh from the citrus, it feels almost light.

Yuzu Tare (makes enough for 4 servings)

155ml Soy Tare (see page 108)

3 tablespoons orange juice

2 tablespoons yuzu juice

35g yuzu koshō

2 tablespoons Negi Oil (see page 105)

30g Blanched Bean Sprouts (see page 118)

20g Soy Bamboo (see page 118)

2 x 25g slices Chashu Pork Belly (see page 123), grilled

2 Nori Squares (see page 120)

Ramen (per serving)

60ml (4 tablespoons) Yuzu Tare (see above), thoroughly mixed

½ teaspoon finely chopped garlic chives

300ml hot Pork Broth (see page 97)

100g straight white tonkotsu noodles, cooked (see page 117)

We've added a few strands of pickled orange zest from the Persimmon Pickle recipe on page 32.

1. To make the Yuzu Tare, mix all the ingredients together well in a bowl.

2. To construct the ramen, put the tare, garlic chives and broth into a hot serving bowl and mix together well. Add the rest of the ingredients in the order above and serve immediately.

Prince of Darkness

This was an idea for some time – a black bowl of pain with a fun name. We love spicy foods and this is the mother of the lot: loads of fresh bird's eyes and habaneros in the tare make it a fiery monster.

Prince of Darkness Tare (makes about 700ml, enough for 10 generous servings)

250ml Soy Tare (see page 108)

50g fresh root ginger, rinsed but not peeled and finely diced

100g Sliced Spring Onions (see page 118)

60g garlic, chopped

2 teaspoons ichimi (Japanese chilli flakes)

1 tablespoon fine Korean chilli powder

50g bird's eye chillies, roughly chopped, including seeds

70g Habanero chillies, roughly chopped, including seeds

40g katsuo bushi (bonito flakes), blitzed to a powder (see page 132)

50ml rice wine vinegar

1 scant tablespoon squid ink

Ramen (per serving)

20g dried wood ear mushrooms

60ml (4 tablespoons) vegetable oil

100g slice of Chashu Pork Belly (see page 123)

70ml Prince of Darkness Tare (see left)

300ml hot Pork Broth (see page 97)

100g straight white tonkotsu noodles, cooked (see page 117)

30g Blanched Bean Sprouts (see page 118)

3-4 fried Padrón peppers (see page 72)

3 tablespoons Mayu (see page 104)

1. To make the Prince of Darkness Tare, blitz all the ingredients together in a blender to a paste. It should be as smooth as possible, so stop the machine regularly and redistribute the ingredients before blending again.

2. Transfer the mixture to a saucepan, set it over a medium heat and warm through, stirring frequently, until the tare just begins to bubble. Remove from the heat and leave to cool. Store in an airtight container in the refrigerator for up to 2 weeks.

3. Put the dried wood ear mushrooms in a bowl and cover with just-boiled water from the kettle. Leave to rehydrate for 20 minutes, then drain well. Cut into 3mm slices.

4. Heat the oil in a small frying pan, add the Chashu Pork Belly slice and fry until crisp and golden on both sides.

5. To construct the ramen, put the tare and broth into a hot serving bowl and mix together well. Add the rest of the ingredients in the order above, adding the pork belly and rehydrated mushrooms after the Bean Sprouts and before the Padrón peppers and Mayu.

Soy Ramen

. . . .

This is our version of a Tokyo ramen with wavy
noodles. This bowl is really brought together by the
Negi Oil on top, which completely changes the dish.

Makes 1 serving

2 tablespoons Soy Tare
(see page 108)

300ml hot Chicken Broth
(see page 102)

1 tablespoon Chicken Fat
(see page 105)

100g Tokyo wavy noodles,
cooked (see page 117)

30g Blanched Bean Sprouts
(see page 118)

2 x 25g slices Chashu Pork
Belly (see page 123)

1 tablespoon diced white
onion

20g Soy Bamboo (see page
118)

1 Marinated Egg, halved
(see page 120)

handful (about 15g) of
mustard leaf

½ tablespoon Negi Oil (see
page 105)

2 Nori Squares (see page
120)

1. Put the tare and broth into a hot serving bowl and mix
together well. Add the rest of the ingredients in the order
above and serve immediately.

T22 Ramen

When we were first writing the original menu we wanted to serve some ramen without pork, to cater for as many Londoners as possible. We came up with a chicken chashu version of a simple Tokyo ramen, Tom picked the number 22 at random and the dish became known as the T22. It is one of the most popular we do, which could be something to do with the Cock Scratchings™.

A note about Cock Scratchings™: Chicken fat is a critical component in a Tokyo ramen. We had a load of chicken skins from our Pulled Chicken and wondered if we could roast those to get roast chicken-skin taste into our chicken fat. After about six hours of roasting in our little oven, we finally had a load of crisp skins and a load of fat. Then, since we had gone to that much effort, we thought let's push it a bit further, crush them up and get them really dry, then season them to use on a ramen. We joked for a few days before we opened about calling them cock scratchings, like the pork scratchings popular in pubs, but thought, 'Nah, we've not worked all these years to have the highlight of our first-ever restaurant be 'cock scratchings''. But, at the last minute, we said, 'Fuck it. Why not?' They have been popular ever since and people add them to all our other ramen as well. Our waiters tell funny stories of how various people interact with them over Cock Scratchings™, so it seems that what started as a kitchen joke has come to be fun for everyone.

Pulled Chicken (makes about 400g)
1kg chicken thighs, skin on, bone in
200ml Soy Tare (see page 108)

Ramen (per serving)
2 tablespoons Soy Tare (see page 108)
300ml hot Chicken Broth (see page 102)

1 tablespoon Chicken Fat (see page 105)
100g Tokyo wavy noodles, cooked (see page 117)
30g Blanched Bean Sprouts (see page 118)
60g Pulled Chicken (see left)
1 tablespoon diced white onion
20g Soy Bamboo (see page 118)

1 Marinated Egg (see page 120), halved
handful (about 15g) of mustard leaf
1 tablespoon Negi Oil (see page 105)
30g Cock Scratchings™ (see page 127)
2 Nori Squares (see page 120)

Continued

T22 Ramen (continued)

1. To make the Pulled Chicken, remove the skin from the chicken thighs and reserve to make Cock Scratchings™ (see page 127). Place the thighs in a single layer in a large saucepan and just cover with water. Set over a low heat and heat slowly to just below boiling point (90°C on a thermometer). Maintain this temperature for 1½ hours, making sure the water level remains constant, topping it up as required. At the end of this time, the meat should be tender and come away easily from the bone. Leave the thighs to cool in the cooking liquid for 30 minutes.

2. Place the base of pan in an ice bath to cool completely, mixing and topping up the ice in the bath regularly.

3. Once cooled, remove the thighs from the cooking liquid, reserving the liquid (see right). Carefully remove the bones and any cartilage and connective tissue from each thigh. Break each thigh down into large strips of meat about 2cm wide. Place the pulled chicken thigh meat in a dish and add the Soy Tare. Mix well and leave to marinate for 5 minutes. Mix well again, then leave to marinate for a further 5 minutes. Transfer the marinated chicken meat to a colander set in the sink and leave to drain thoroughly.

4. The chicken is now ready to use or eat. It can be stored, covered, in the refrigerator for up to 3 days.

5. To construct the ramen, put the tare and broth into a hot serving bowl and mix together well. Add the rest of the ingredients in the order listed and serve immediately.

Use the chicken cooking liquid to make Chicken Broth (see page 102), adding it to the pan at the outset in place of some of the water.

Slurping
as you eat
allows the noodles
to cool quickly
so you don't
burn your mouth.

Tantanmen Ramen

Originally inspired by dan dan mien, a noodle dish from Sichuan in China, this is a relative newcomer to the ramen scene in Japan. The tare is based on *goma*, or sesame paste, but also calls for a lot of chilli oil. Some shops in Japan also add some Sichuan peppercorns to it for their tongue-numbing effect. The mince includes Japanese tobanjan (fermented hot bean paste) to fry off. The original version is made from pork but the London version is the Tantanmen 2 with chicken and chicken mince (see page 170).

We probably have had more queries about this dish than any other, simply because people do not understand it. Generally people think the richness is from peanut butter, although there are no peanuts in it. People also don't understand the amount of chilli oil we put in, in an effort to respect the original versions.

Spicy Pork Mince (makes 4 servings)

1 teaspoon Chilli Oil (see page 104)

1 teaspoon vegetable oil

200g minced pork

20g tobanjan (Chinese hot bean sauce)

75ml soy sauce

1 teaspoon finely chopped garlic

1 teaspoon finely chopped fresh root ginger

½ a spring onion, finely chopped

Ramen (per serving)

90g Goma Tare (see page 112)

300ml hot Chicken Broth (see page 102)

100g cooked straight white tonkotsu noodles (see page 117)

30g Blanched Bean Sprouts (see page 118)

20g Soy Bamboo (see page 118)

1 Marinated Egg (see page 120), halved

45g Spicy Pork Mince (see above)

1 large pak choi leaf, blanched, drained and chilled

1 x 25g Chashu Pork Belly Slice (see page 123)

2g garlic shoots, very finely chopped

0.5g (tiny pinch) ito togarashi (angel hair chilli), or to taste

Chilli Oil (see page 104), to taste

1. To make the Spicy Pork Mince (remember that this is enough for 4 servings), heat both oils in a wok or frying pan and stir-fry the minced pork until browned. Add the other ingredients and continue cooking until the mixture is dry. Set aside.

2. To construct the ramen, add the tare and broth to a hot serving bowl and whisk together very thoroughly until the tare has made the broth creamy, then whisk some more!

3. Add the cooked noodles, then top with the Bean Sprouts, Soy Bamboo, Marinated Egg halves, one-quarter of the spicy pork mince, the pak choi and garlic shoots. Finish with as much ito togarashi and Chilli Oil as you dare before serving.

Tantanmen 2 Ramen

There are plenty of people who don't eat pork. We still wanted them to enjoy one of the newer forms of ramen in Japan, so we swapped in some chicken to make Tantanmen 2.

Spicy Chicken Mince (makes 4 servings)

1 teaspoon Chilli Oil (see page 104)

1 teaspoon vegetable oil

200g minced chicken

20g tobanjan (Chinese hot bean sauce)

75ml soy sauce

1 teaspoon finely chopped garlic

1 teaspoon finely chopped fresh root ginger

½ a spring onion, finely chopped

Ramen (per serving)

90g Goma Tare (see page 112)

300ml hot Chicken Broth (see page 102)

100g cooked straight white tonkotsu noodles (see page 117)

30g Blanched Bean Sprouts (see page 118)

20g Soy Bamboo (see page 118)

1 Marinated Egg (see page 120), halved

45g Spicy Chicken Mince (see left)

1 large pak choi leaf, blanched, drained and chilled

30g Pulled Chicken (see page 164)

2g garlic shoots, very finely chopped

0.5g (tiny pinch) ito togarashi (angel hair chilli), or to taste

Chilli Oil (see page 104), to taste

1. To make the Spicy Chicken Mince (remember that this is enough for 4 servings), heat both oils in a wok or frying pan and stir-fry the minced chicken until browned. Add the other ingredients and continue cooking until the mixture is dry. Set aside.

2. To construct the ramen, add the tare and broth to a hot serving bowl and whisk together very thoroughly until the tare has made the broth creamy, then whisk some more!

3. Add the cooked noodles, then top with the Bean Sprouts, Soy Bamboo, Marinated Egg halves, one-quarter of the spicy chicken mince, the pak choi and garlic shoots. Finish with as much ito togarashi and Chilli Oil as you dare before serving.

Spicy Miso Ramen

Miso ramen is most popular in Sapporo and, because we always wanted to reflect a variety of styles, we put this on our menu about nine months after we opened. Now it is the one we love to eat most often. This was the first time we used pork neck chashu on our ramen, then – for some freshness – we fried some Padrón peppers and put them on whole. Padrón are not too foreign to Japanese cooking as they eat a lot of shishito peppers, which are a hybrid of the Spanish Padrón and the jalapeño from Mexico, in Japan. This is a great example of how Japan's food culture is evolving.

Makes 1 serving

75g Spicy Miso Tare (see page 109)

300ml hot Chicken Broth (see page 102)

100g straight white tonkotsu noodles, cooked (see page 117)

30g Blanched Bean Sprouts (see page 118)

20g Soy Bamboo (see page 118)

1 Marinated Egg (see page 120), halved

80g Chashu Pork Neck (see page 123), thickly sliced

20g fried Padrón peppers (see page 72)

1 spring onion, sliced

pinch of ito togarashi (angel hair chilli), or to taste

1 tablespoon sesame oil

1 tablespoon Chilli Oil (see page 104)

1. Add the tare and broth to a hot serving bowl and whisk together very thoroughly to ensure an even taste.

2. Add the cooked noodles and top with the Bean Sprouts, Soy Bamboo, Marinated Egg halves, Chashu Pork Neck, fried Padrón peppers, sliced spring onion, ito togarashi, sesame oil and Chilli Oil, then serve immediately. Be sure to serve this ramen piping hot.

Curry Ramen

Curry is typical of *yoshoku* (foreign Japanese foods) and has been in Japan now for a little over a hundred years. Although people know katsu curry, this familiarity just comes from an instant packet that is full of MSG. We go to the trouble of making a curry base that is uniquely made fruity with bananas and apples; this is then made into a tare for the ramen but, with the addition of just a bit more flour, it also works well as a curry sauce. The fried chicken is also very tasty when it goes a little soggy.

Makes 1 serving

50g Hispi (sweetheart or pointed) cabbage, quartered, cored and cut into 2.5cm squares

90ml Curry Tare (see page 115)

300ml hot Chicken Broth (see page 102)

100g Tokyo wavy noodles, cooked (see page 117)

6 pieces (about 105g) Fried Chicken Kara-age (see page 60)

6 (about 50g) fried Padrón peppers (see page 72)

2½ tablespoons Chilli Oil (see page 104)

½ tablespoon Negi Oil (see page 105)

1. Blanch the Hispi cabbage in a saucepan of boiling water for 5 seconds, then drain immediately.

2. To construct the ramen, add the tare and broth to a hot serving bowl and whisk together very thoroughly. Top with the remaining ramen ingredients in the order above, adding the cabbage after the chicken. Serve immediately.

Sour Pepper Ramen

When we first tried out this recipe, it reminded us a bit of a tom yum-style Thai soup but, when we were discussing the toppings, we felt it needed to reflect something very common in South East Asia – the mix of seafood and meat. So we fried some salmon and put it with some pork. If we had owned a better kitchen, we may have pan roasted the salmon instead, but restrictions have driven our menu many times and good things have come from that.

Sour Pepper Tare (makes 320ml, enough for 10 servings)

215ml Soy Tare (see page 108)

100ml lemon juice

½ teaspoon toasted ground black pepper (see below)

½ teaspoon toasted ground white pepper (see below)

½ teaspoon Korean chilli powder

1 teaspoon bonito powder (see page 132)

½ teaspoon Maldon sea salt

Ramen (per serving)

40g Chashu Pork Neck (see page 123), thickly sliced

60ml (4 tablespoons) Sour Pepper Tare (see left)

1 tablespoon Chicken Fat (see page 105)

300ml hot Chicken Broth (see page 102)

100g straight white tonkotsu noodles, cooked (see page 117)

½ a Sliced Spring Onion (see page 118)

1 teaspoon diced white onion

½ tablespoon unsalted butter

pinch of toasted white sesame seeds

30g Blanched Bean Sprouts (see page 118)

20g Soy Bamboo (see page 118)

25g trimmed spring onion, blanched for 5 seconds, drained and dried well, then fairly well charred with a blowtorch or in a smoking hot griddle pan

¼ lemon, charred with a blowtorch or over a gas flame until fairly well charred

50g Salmon Kara-age, thickly cut (see page 62)

1 tablespoon Negi Oil (see page 105)

1 Marinated Egg (see page 120), halved

1. To make the Sour Pepper Tare, mix all the ingredients together thoroughly. Store in an airtight container in the refrigerator for up to 2 days.

2. Lightly char the Chashu Pork Neck slices with a blowtorch or in a smoking-hot griddle pan or under a hot grill.

3. To construct the ramen, put the tare, fat and broth into a hot serving bowl and mix together well. Add the rest of the ingredients in the order above, adding the charred pork slices after the Bean Sprouts and before the Soy Bamboo. Serve immediately.

For the toasted black and white pepper, gently toast the whole peppercorns in a dry frying pan, then grind with a pestle and mortar.

Sweet 3 Miso Ramen

We opened with this on our menu. The idea was that, judging by the tons of black cod Ross served at Nobu and Zuma, people love sweet miso, so let's blend three of them to make a sweet three-miso tare. We wanted to make sure it wasn't confused with the miso ramen so typical of Sapporo, although we did take some inspiration from there. Hokkaido is the only area of Japan that is famous for dairy products, There they typically top their miso ramen with slices of butter and canned corn. We do serve butter on this one but blowtorch some fresh corn to add to ours too.

Sweet 3 Miso Tare (makes 275g, enough for 4 servings with a little left over)
50g shinshu (yellow) miso
25g akadashi (red) miso
75g mugi (barley) miso
125ml mirin

Ramen (per serving)
5g dried wakame
60g Sweet 3 Miso Tare (see left)
300ml hot Chicken Broth (see page 102)
100g straight white tonkotsu noodles, cooked (see page 117)
30g Blanched Bean Sprouts (see page 118)
20g Soy Bamboo (see page 118)

2 strips Roasted Sweetcorn (see page 127)
60g Pulled Chicken (see page 164)
1 Marinated Egg (see page 120), halved
1-2 garlic shoots, finely sliced
20g unsalted butter
1 tablespoon Negi Oil (see page 105)

1. To make the Sweet 3 Miso Tare, mix all the ingredients together thoroughly in a bowl.

2. Put the wakame in a bowl (remember that this is for a single serving only, so multiply this quantity and those of the other ramen ingredients according to how many ramen servings you are making) and cover with just-boiled water from the kettle. Leave to rehydrate for 15–20 minutes, then drain well.

3. To construct the ramen, put the tare and broth into a hot serving bowl and mix together well. Add the rest of the ingredients in the order above, adding the rehydrated wakame after the Soy Bamboo.

Tripe & Chorizo Ramen

We challenged one of our chefs, Loic, to take inspiration from his recent trip to Spain to recreate the Spanish tripe stew he had raved about and turn it into a ramen. It was a good challenge and I think we came up with a worthy dish.

Tripe Sauce (makes about 750ml)

125ml olive oil

3 small garlic cloves, roughly chopped

½ small white onion, diced

210g chorizo sausage, skinned and cut into large batons

620g tripe, rinsed, drained and cut into large pieces

2 x 400g cans peeled plum tomatoes

60ml (4 tablespoons) sake

2 tablespoons Chicken Broth (see page 102)

1 tablespoon Maldon sea salt

¾ teaspoon hot paprika

¾ teaspoon sweet paprika

Tripe Tare (makes enough for 8 servings)

125g Soy Tare (see page 108)

1 tablespoon Shio Tare (see page 108)

375ml Tripe Sauce (see above)

Paprika Mix

½ teaspoon hot paprika

½ teaspoon sweet paprika

Ramen (per serving)

90ml Tripe Tare (see left)

300ml hot Chicken Broth (see page 102)

100g straight white tonkotsu noodles, cooked (see page 117)

30g Blanched Bean Sprouts (see page 118)

2 fried Padrón peppers (see page 72)

4 pieces chorizo sausage, from making the Tripe Sauce (see left)

4-5 pieces tripe, from making the Tripe Sauce (see left)

¼ teaspoon Paprika Mix (see above)

2 spring onions, blanched in boiling water for 10 seconds, drained and dried well then fairly well charred with a blowtorch or in a smoking-hot griddle pan

1 tablespoon chorizo oil, reserved from making the Tripe Sauce (see left)

Continued

Tripe & Chorizo Ramen (continued)

1. Put the olive oil, garlic and onion in large saucepan and cook over a medium heat for 5 minutes without colouring. Add the chorizo and cook for 15 minutes, stirring frequently and being careful not to let the mixture scorch. Strain the contents of the pan through a sieve, reserving both the solids and the chorizo-infused oil.

2. Return half the oil to the pan and set over a medium heat. Add the tripe and cook until the water from the tripe is reduced down level with the tripe – it will expel a lot of water.

3. Stir in the canned tomatoes, sake, Chicken Broth, Maldon sea salt, both types of paprika and the reserved chorizo, onion and garlic mixture and cook for 2–3 hours over a low–medium heat, stirring frequently, until the tripe is tender.

4. Remove the chorizo and tripe, setting them aside for the ramen, then reduce the sauce a little further, if necessary, until you are left with a volume of about 750ml. Blitz in a blender or food processor until completely smooth.

5. To make the Triple Tare, mix the Soy Tare and Shio Tare into the Tripe Sauce.

6. Meanwhile, quickly fry the cooked chorizo in a nonstick frying pan on all sides until crisp. Cut the cooked tripe into smaller strips, as shown in the photo on page 181, and reheat ready to top the ramen.

7. Mix together both types of paprika to make the Paprika Mix.

8. To construct the ramen, put the tare and broth into a hot serving bowl and mix together well. Add the rest of the ingredients in the order listed, adding the fried Padrón peppers, chorizo and tripe in that order after the Bean Sprouts and before the spring onions. Serve immediately.

Globally ramen is
constantly evolving,
even in Japan.

BLTEC Ramen
(Bacon, Lettuce, Tomato, Egg & Cheese)

We created this ramen probably a few months after opening. We had a young Japanese girl working with us at the time who was shocked by the idea of a cheese ramen because she thought it was not very Japanese. We asked her to check the internet and she then realized that cheese ramen was something that was happening in Japan and accepted it, though many of our customers were also surprised by it. The key thing with this bowl is to make sure it is eaten very fast, as it become a bit too thick otherwise.

Mizuna Pesto (makes 150g, enough for 10 servings)

100g mizuna, roughly chopped

50ml olive oil

½ garlic clove, peeled

½ teaspoon Maldon sea salt

Tare (makes 4 servings)

3 large eggs

1 teaspoon vegetable oil

150g thick-cut dry-cured streaky bacon, cut into batons, or use lardons

8 egg yolks

65ml Shio Tare (see page 108)

170g Parmesan cheese, finely grated, plus extra to taste

½ tablespoon Maldon sea salt

½ tablespoon freshly ground black pepper

Ramen (per serving)

120ml Tare (see left)

300ml hot Chicken Broth (see page 102)

100g straight white tonkotsu noodles, cooked (see page 117)

1 tomato, halved, then a thin slice cut from 1 half, other half reserved for squeezing

1 tablespoon Mizuna Pesto (see left)

25g crispy bacon pieces, reserved from making the tare (see left)

small handful of mizuna leaves

Continued

RAMEN

BLTEC Ramen (continued)

1. To make the Mizuna Pesto, blitz all the ingredients together in a blender until smooth. Store in an airtight container in the refrigerator for up 4 days.

2. For the Tare, bring a small saucepan of water to the boil, gently lower in the whole eggs and simmer for 5 minutes. Drain, refresh under cold running water and shell, then discard the whites. Set the softly boiled egg yolks aside.

3. Heat the oil in a frying pan and gently fry the bacon batons (or lardons) until they begin to give up their fat. Increase the heat slightly and continue to cook, stirring frequently, until the bacon is golden and very crisp. Remove from the pan with a slotted spoon and drain on kitchen paper. Measure out 50g bacon fat from the pan to use in the tare.

4. Once cooled, blitz the bacon batons into fine, crispy pieces.

5. Blitz the remaining tare ingredients, including the reserved bacon fat and the soft-boiled egg yolks, in a powerful blender until a smooth paste is formed (the black pepper will stay a little coarse).

6. To construct the ramen, put the tare and broth into a hot serving bowl and mix together well. Top with the noodles and the tomato slice, then squeeze over the juice and pulp from the remaining tomato half. Finish with the pesto, the crispy bacon and the mizuna leaves. Serve immediately.

187 In the Bone Daddies Kitchen:
Making our chilli oil and chilli bits

Thai Ramen

A fleeting trip to Thailand inspired us to come up with this ramen, as simple and satisfying as they come. Our challenge was to re-create the moreish balance of sweet, sour, salty and fresh that we'd tasted there. We don't often focus on keeping our ramen really simple, but this was the result of trying more than 30 different bowls using a few simple fresh ingredients.

Thai Tare (makes 125ml, enough for 4 servings)
90ml Soy Tare (see page 108)
35ml fish sauce, ideally Squid brand

Ramen (per serving)
1 tablespoon finely sliced red onion
2 tablespoons Thai Tare (see above)
300ml hot Chicken Broth (see page 102)

100g Tokyo wavy noodles, cooked (see page 117)
2 lime quarters
½ medium tomato, deseeded and cut into 1cm dice
½ green chilli, finely sliced
½ tablespoon finely sliced coriander root and/or stem
2g (large pinch) Chilli Bits (see page 129)
20g Soy Bamboo (see page 118)
50g Pulled Chicken (see page 164)

a few picked coriander leaves
½ tablespoon Negi Oil (see page 105)

1. To make the Thai Tare, put the ingredients in a bowl and mix together well.

2. For the ramen, put the sliced red onion in a bowl and cover with cold water. Leave to soak for 15 minutes, then rinse thoroughly and drain.

3. To construct the ramen, put the tare and broth into a hot serving bowl and mix together well. Add the rest of the ingredients in the order above, squeezing the juice from the lime quarters into the bowl and adding the drained red onion at the end. Serve immediately.

Tomato & Chorizo Ramen

I think the same trip that resulted in the Tripe & Chorizo Ramen on page 180 also spawned this recipe, as we were really exploring Spain to find new ingredients for ramen.

Tomato & Chorizo Tare (makes about 320g, enough for 5 generous servings)

110g mugi (barley) miso

175g sun-dried tomatoes

4 teaspoons Shio Tare (see page 108)

4 teaspoons Soy Tare (see page 108)

Fried Chorizo (per serving)

1 good-quality mini picante chorizo sausage, peeled

2 tablespoons vegetable oil

Ramen (per serving)

60g Tomato and Chorizo Tare (see left)

300ml hot Chicken Broth (see page 102)

100g straight white tonkotsu noodles, cooked (see page 117)

30g Blanched Bean Sprouts (see page 118)

15g (small handful) mustard leaves

½ tablespoon diced white onion, soaked in cold water for 15 minutes, then rinsed and patted dry

3 slices Fried Chorizo (see left)

1 tablespoon chorizo oil, reserved from the Fried Chorizo (see left)

1. To make the Tomato and Chorizo Tare, blitz all the ingredients together with 4 teaspoons of water in a food processor until almost smooth.

2. Cut the mini chorizo lengthways into thirds. Heat the oil in a frying pan over a medium-high heat, add the chorizo and fry on both sides, allowing some of the oil to render and achieving a good colour on each side. Reserve the chorizo oil for the ramen and reheat the chorizo before serving.

3. To construct the ramen, put the tare and broth into a hot serving bowl and mix together well. Add the rest of the ingredients in the order above and serve immediately.

Dipping Ramen

As we are in London, from the beginning we have aimed to keep everything possible on the menu in English, rather than in Japanese so, rather than describe this as *tsukemen*, we called it a 'dipping ramen'. People still pour the 'sauce' over the top, despite the clue being in the name, but, hey, so long as they enjoy themselves.

This soup is a lot stronger than our usual soups, so that when you dip the toppings in it, it gives a nice savoury coating to each bite. Some people (like me!) are happy to drink the soup as it is; alternatively, adding extra chicken broth will make it less salty.

Makes 1 serving

Soup
2 tablespoons Soy Tare (see page 108)
½ a Sliced Spring Onion (see page 118)
1 teaspoon Chicken Fat (see page 105)
130ml hot Chicken Broth (see page 102)
1 teaspoon Negi Oil (see page 105)

Noodles & Toppings
100g uncooked Tokyo wavy noodles
3 x 25g slices Chashu Pork Belly (see page 123)
1 Marinated Egg (see page 120), halved
40g Blanched Bean Sprouts (see page 118)

30g Soy Bamboo (see page 118)
3½ Sliced Spring Onions (see page 118)
½ tablespoon Negi Oil (see page 105)
large pinch of kizami nori (shredded nori)

1. First, prepare the noodles by cooking in boiling water for twice as long as usual (see page 117), then drain and immediately plunge into iced water. Mix thoroughly to remove the excess starch and evenly chill. Once chilled, drain well.

2. To make the soup, put the Soy Tare, Sliced Spring Onion, Chicken Fat and Negi Oil into a hot serving bowl, add the hot Chicken Broth and mix.

3. Serve the noodles with the toppings in the order above, with the soup on the side.

Kimchi Ramen

Most of our chicken broth ramen would work equally well with fish broth. We originally made our kimchi ramen with fish broth, but have since been doing it with chicken. This was inspired by the kimchi *nabe* (stews) we have had over the years and love, and it's also a popular style in Japan.

King Prawns (makes 4 servings)
200g peeled and deveined raw king prawns
50g potato flour
1 litre rapeseed oil, for deep-frying

Mussels (makes 4 servings)
1.2 litres hot Chicken Broth (see page 102)
200g fresh mussels, scrubbed and debearded

Ramen (per serving)
70g Kimchi Tare (see page 112)
300ml hot Chicken Broth (see page 102), reserved from blanching mussels
100g straight white tonkotsu noodles, cooked (see page 117)
30g Blanched Bean Sprouts (see page 118)
40g Soy Bamboo (see page 118)
1 Marinated Egg (see page 120), halved
40g Kimchi (see page 30)
1 Sliced Spring Onion (see page 118)

2 strips (about 40g) Roasted Sweetcorn (see page 127)
50g (small handful) Mussels (see left)
50g (about 2) King Prawns (see left)
1 tablespoon Negi Oil (see page 105)
Chilli Oil, to taste (see page 104)
¼ green chilli, finely sliced

1. Mix the king prawns in the potato flour until evenly coated.

2. Pour the oil into a deep saucepan (at least 2 litres in capacity) and set over a medium-high heat. When the oil reaches 180°C on a thermometer, deep-fry the coated prawns for 1 minute until just cooked through. Remove with a slotted spoon and drain thoroughly on kitchen paper.

3. Heat the chicken broth in a pan. Add the mussels and blanch for 90 seconds. Remove from the broth and set aside.

4. To construct the ramen, put the tare and broth into a hot serving bowl and mix together well. Add the rest of the ingredients in the order above. Serve immediately.

Mushroom Ramen

We didn't have a vegetarian ramen on the menu when we opened, but then we never thought vegetarians would even enter a Bone Daddies. We were wrong, so we aimed to make a ramen that was incredibly 'meaty' without the meat. A few guys in the team participated in the development of this one and the result is a rich and deeply savoury ramen. The Shin-yokohama Raumen Museum of Japan actually tasted our mushroom ramen and said that it was the best example of vegetarian ramen they had ever eaten. Even in Japan. Ramen chefs in Japan haven't got such delicious tastes in their vegetarian ramen as we have in ours – they said.

Mushrooms (makes 4 servings)

5 tablespoons vegetable oil, or as needed

500g hon shimeji mushrooms, ends trimmed and broken into small bunches

8 medium field mushrooms, stems discarded, peeled and cut into wedges

3 large garlic cloves, peeled and finely sliced

6 sprigs of thyme

Maldon sea salt, to taste

Ramen (per serving)

1 asparagus spear, woody base trimmed

25g pak choi, leaves separated

2 tablespoons Soy Tare (see page 108), plus 1 tablespoon for marinating the tofu

15g drained silken tofu, cut into 1cm dice

1 tablespoon Mayu (see page 104)

2 garlic shoots, sliced 1–2mm thick

300ml hot Mushroom Broth (see page 101)

100g straight white tonkotsu noodles, cooked (see page 117)

30g Blanched Bean Sprouts (see page 118)

1 Marinated Egg, halved (see page 120)

30g sliced Soy-braised Shiitake (see page 129), heated through

1 serving cooked hon shimeji (see left and method overleaf)

1 serving cooked field mushrooms (see left and method overleaf)

½ tablespoon mushroom oil, reserved from frying the mushrooms (see left and method overleaf)

1 slice Mushroom Butter (see page 105)

Continued

Mushroom Ramen (continued)

1. First, cook the 2 types of mushroom in separate frying pans. Cover the base of each pan with half the vegetable oil and place both over a medium-high heat. Add the hon shimeji mushrooms to one pan and the field mushrooms to the other and cook for a few minutes until coloured on all sides. When almost cooked, add half the garlic and thyme to each pan, adding more oil if necessary. Sauté for a further 1–2 minutes and season well with sea salt. Remove the mushrooms from the pans and drain on kitchen paper. Keep warm for serving, reserving the mushroom oil.

2. For the ramen, start by blanching the asparagus (remember to blanch as many spears as needed according to how many people you are serving – you will need one spear per portion of ramen) in plenty of boiling water for 1 minute. Remove with a slotted spoon and immediately plunge into iced water. Drain, cut the spear into thirds and set aside.

3. Blanch the pak choi in the boiling water for 5 seconds. Remove with a slotted spoon and plunge into iced water, then drain. Drain and plunge into iced water, then drain again.

4. Sprinkle the extra Soy Tare over the tofu (1 tablespoon per 15g portion) and leave to marinate for 1 minute, then drain.

5. To construct the ramen, add half the Mayu, the remaining 2 tablespoons Soy Tare and the garlic shoots to a hot serving bowl, then add the hot Mushroom Broth and mix gently. Top with the remaining ingredients in the order above, adding the asparagus, pak choi and the drained tofu cubes after the cooked mushrooms, finishing with the remaining ½ tablespoon Mayu.

Ramen doesn't have
that history that washoku has,
so it's always been
whatever the chef
wants it to be.

3

Mazemen, Aburamen & Hiyashi Chuka

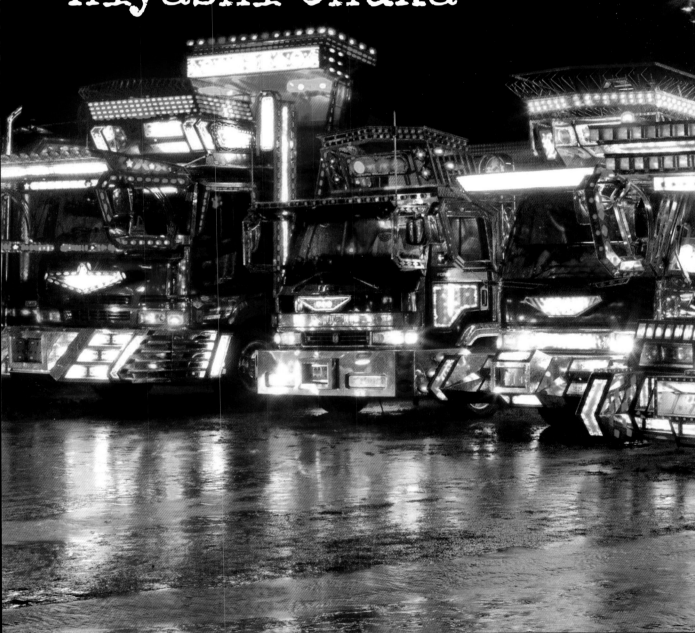

Chilled Chilli Ramen

More Sichuan Chinese inspiration, like the recipe on page 168, this covers our need for spice but also sits nicely as summer ramen.

Chilli Dashi Sauce (makes about 700ml, enough for 4 generous servings)

60ml (4 tablespoons) Chicken Broth (see page 102), cooked until reduced to 1 tablespoon

300ml Dashi (see page 108)

110ml light soy sauce

80ml mirin

65ml rice wine vinegar

2 tablespoons Chilli Bits (see page 129), or use red chilli flakes

2 tablespoons sesame oil

2 teaspoons Chinese black vinegar

1½ teaspoons bonito powder (see page 132)

2 bird's eye chillies, very finely sliced

1 garlic clove, finely chopped

Ramen (per serving)

100g Tokyo wavy noodles (see page 117)

80g deseeded cucumber, sliced into 5mm julienne

50g Spicy Chicken Mince (see page 170)

160ml Chilli Dashi Sauce (see left)

large pinch of toasted white sesame seeds, plus an extra pinch to serve

2 Sliced Spring Onions (see page 118)

½ green chilli, finely sliced

1-2 birds' eye chillies, finely sliced

1 tablespoon Garlic Chips (see page 128)

1 whole Marinated Egg (see page 120)

2 Nori Squares (see page 120)

1. To make the Chilli Dashi Sauce, mix all the ingredients together well in a bowl with 65ml of water. Cover and chill in the refrigerator until ready to serve.

2. Prepare the noodles by cooking in boiling water for twice as long as usual (see page 117), then drain and immediately plunge into iced water. Mix thoroughly to remove the excess starch and evenly chill. Once chilled, drain well.

3. Place a mixing bowl over ice, and when chilled, add the noodles, cucumber, Spicy Chicken Mince, Chilli Dashi Sauce, the large pinch of sesame seeds and the Sliced Spring Onion. Mix well to combine evenly, then transfer to a chilled serving bowl.

4. Top with the chillies, Garlic Chips, Marinated Egg, the extra pinch of sesame seeds and the Nori Squares, and serve immediately.

Ramen Salad MkII

Hiyashi Chuka is a chilled ramen-style 'salad', which is typically a cold ramen with a dressing rather than a broth. This one is not that different to those you might find in Japan. It's very refreshing.

Hiyashi Chuka (makes 640ml, enough for 4 servings)

200ml light soy sauce

120ml rice wine vinegar

2 teaspoons sesame oil

100g caster sugar

120ml Chicken Broth (see page 102), cooked until reduced to 1 tablespoon

large pinch of katsuo bushi (bonito flakes)

large pinch of Maldon sea salt, or to taste

Omelette (makes 4 servings)

3 eggs

large pinch of Maldon sea salt

vegetable oil, for frying

Ramen (per serving)

100g uncooked straight white tonkostu noodles

1 fine asparagus spear, woody base trimmed

20g carrot, julienned

½ tomato, cut into wedges

2 strips of Roasted Sweetcorn (see page 127)

50g Omelette (see left)

60g Pulled Chicken (see page 164)

15g mizuna

1 Sliced Spring Onion (see page 118)

30g Blanched Bean Sprouts (see page 118)

160ml Hiyashi Chuka (see left)

Continued

Ramen Salad MkII (continued)

1. To make the Hiyashi Chuka, combine all the ingredients in a saucepan with 120ml of water and bring just to the boil, then turn off the heat and leave to cool. Strain through a fine-mesh sieve lined with muslin. Transfer to an airtight container and chill in the refrigerator, where it will keep for up to a week.

2. To make the omelette, whisk the eggs thoroughly in a bowl and season with the sea salt. Wipe the inside of a nonstick pan with a little vegetable oil and heat over medium-high heat. Pour a little of the egg mixture into the pan, tilting the pan to fully cover its base with a 2–3mm layer. Briefly cook until just set – we blowtorch the top to speed things up. Tip out on to a chopping board and leave to cool. Repeat with the remaining egg mixture. Stack the omelettes one top of another, then roll into a cigar shape and slice thinly across. The omelette is now ready to use.

3. For the ramen, prepare the noodles by cooking in boiling water for twice as long as usual (see page 117), then drain and immediately plunge into iced water. Mix thoroughly to remove the excess starch and evenly chill. Once chilled, drain well.

4. Blanch the asparagus in plenty of boiling water for 1 minute 20 seconds. Remove with a slotted spoon and immediately plunge into iced water. Drain, cut each spear into thirds and set aside.

5. Put the cooled noodles into a chilled bowl and arrange all the toppings, except the Hiyashi Chuka, so that no vegetable covers another. Then cover all over with the Hiyashi Chuka and serve.

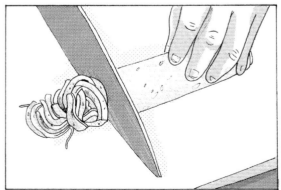

Ox Heart Mazemen

Mazemen is a soupless ramen which is packed with flavour. Instead of a soup it has more of a 'sauce', in the same way that spaghetti has a sauce in Italian food. This one is delicious and rich, and the fresh chillies give it a good lift.

Ox Heart (makes enough for 5 ramen, including the Tomato Sauce)

675g ox heart, with a good amount of extra fat (200g) on the outside

Tomato Sauce (makes about 1kg, enough for 5 generous servings)

500ml olive oil

1 white onion, roughly chopped

8 garlic cloves, roughly chopped

1 fresh bay leaf

¼ bunch of thyme

ox heart trimmings (see page 208)

3 x 400g cans peeled plum tomatoes, blitzed until smooth

Mazeman (per serving)

60g diced ox heart (see page 208)

3 tablespoons Chicken Fat (see page 105)

5 fine green beans, topped and tailed

5 sugar snap peas, topped and tailed

1 tomato, cut into 12 pieces

90ml Tomato Sauce (see left)

2 tablespoons Soy Tare (see page 108)

100g straight white tonkotsu noodles, cooked (see page 117)

2 tablespoons finely grated Parmesan cheese

1 green chilli, finely sliced

2 slices (about 30g in total) ox heart sashimi

Maldon sea salt

← Continued

Ox Heart Mazemen (continued)

1. First, prepare the ox heart. Remove the fat, the tough outer and inner layers and blood vessels, setting these trimmings aside to make the Tomato Sauce. Cut the trimmed ox heart into 2 even 3–4cm blocks and cut each block into slices 5–6mm thick, reserving all offcuts. Dice these offcuts into 1cm cubes. Keep the prepared ox heart slices and dice chilled in the refrigerator until required.

2. To make the Tomato Sauce, put the olive oil, onion, garlic, bay leaf, thyme, ox heart trimmings and fat into a saucepan and cook gently for 10 minutes. Add the blitzed canned tomatoes, cover with a lid and cook very gently for 3 hours, stirring frequently, until the mixture is rich and thick.

3. Remove and discard the ox heart trimmings, thyme stems and bay leaf with tongs, then blitz the remaining mixture in a blender until smooth. Carefully strain through a fine chinois or fine-mesh sieve to make a rich, smooth tomato ragú. This will keep, covered, in the refrigerator for up to 4 days.

4. Just before serving, preheat the grill to high or place a griddle pan over the highest heat until smoking hot.

5. Add the reserved diced ox heart to a hot sauté pan with 1 tablespoon of the Chicken Fat and cook for 10 seconds to colour quickly, then add the green beans, sugar snaps and fresh tomato pieces and cook for 10 seconds. Stir in the tomato sauce and 1 tablespoon of the Soy Tare and bring to the boil.

6. At the same time, add the hot noodles and the remaining Chicken Fat and Soy Tare to a hot mixing bowl, mix well and keep hot.

7. Add the noodle mixture to the ox heart, bean and tomato pan, remove from the heat and mix well. Transfer the mixture to a hot serving bowl and add the Parmesan and sliced green chilli.

8. Season the reserved ox heart slices with sea salt, then grill for 15 seconds on each side, or sear in the smoking-hot griddle pan for the same amount of time, and add to the bowl to finish.

Sing Mai Mazemen

Inspired by a Singapore noodle, but without the curry powder, there is a good bit of chilli in this. It's not very pretty but it tastes great!

Makes 1 serving

Noodles

100g straight white tonkotsu noodles, cooked (see page 117)

1 tablespoon Soy Tare (see page 108)

1 tablespoon Chicken Fat (see page 105)

2 tablespoons Chilli Oil (see page 104)

40g Roasted Sweetcorn (see page 127), separated into kernals

1 small carrot, sliced into fine julienne

1 small Sliced Spring Onion (see page 118)

Spicy Scrambled Eggs

1 tablespoon Chicken Fat (see page 105)

1½ tablespoon garlic shoots, sliced 2mm thick

½ green chilli, sliced

80g Spicy Pork Mince (see page 168)

2 eggs, well beaten, then strained through a fine-mesh sieve.

1. Cook the noodles in boiling water for 20 seconds, then drain well and place in a bowl. Add all the remaining noodle ingredients and mix into the noodles. Keep warm.

2. Heat up a pan over a medium-high heat, add the Chicken Fat, garlic shoots, chilli slices and Spicy Pork Mince and quickly sauté for 20–30 seconds.

3. Pour the eggs into the pan and allow to cook a little, then stir to turn the spicy egg mixture into chunky scrambled eggs.

4. Add the spicy scrambled egg mixture to the noodle mixture and fold in well before serving.

Mr Mazemen 2.0

This one is rich – the bacon cream is the base, the mentaiko goes great with the bacon and the cabbage offers different crunch. It would also work well with pasta.

Cream Tare (makes 4 servings)

600ml double cream

6 garlic cloves, roughly chopped

70ml Shio Tare (see page 108)

100g smoked bacon or pancetta trimmings

Paprika Mentaiko Mix (makes 4 servings)

50g mentaiko (seasoned cod's roe), eggs carefully removed from the membrane

very small pinch of hot smoked paprika

20ml grapeseed oil

Crispy Bacon Batons and Rind (makes 4 servings)

250g rind-on dry-cured bacon in one piece, any cartilage removed

1 tablespoon vegetable oil, plus 1 litre for deep-frying

Mazemen (per serving)

190ml Cream Tare (see left)

160g straight white tonkotsu noodles, cooked (see page 117)

1 tablespoon bacon fat, reserved from frying the bacon (see above)

Chilli Oil (see page 104), to taste

1 tablespoon Paprika Mentaiko Mix (see left)

1 large Sliced Spring Onion (see page 118)

Toppings (per serving)

80g white cabbage, finely sliced, then rinsed in iced water and drained to make it crisp

1 large Sliced Spring Onion (see page 118)

1 tablespoon Paprika Mentaiko Mix (see left)

1 tablespoon Chilli Oil (see page 104)

2 tablespoons Crispy Bacon Batons (see left)

1 piece Crispy Bacon Rind (see left)

← ——— Continued

Mr Mazemen 2.0 (continued)

1. To make the Cream Tare, combine all the ingredients in a saucepan over a medium heat and gently simmer, stirring frequently, for 20 minutes, trying not to reduce the volume too much. Strain through a fine-mesh sieve to remove the flavourings.

2. To make the Paprika Mentaiko Mix, mix the mentaiko eggs and paprika together until evenly combined and coloured. Then gently mix in the grapeseed oil. The mixture can be stored in an airtight container in the refrigerator for up to 3 days.

3. To make the Bacon Batons and Rind, cut the bacon into 5mm-thick slices. Carefully remove the rind from the bacon slices along with about the same width of fat with one cut, so that you have long strips with half fat to rind on each. Set aside.

4. Slice the rest of the bacon into 5mm batons. Heat the 1 tablespoon vegetable oil in a frying pan over a medium heat and gently fry the bacon batons, stirring frequently, until very crisp. Drain through a sieve, reserving all the rendered bacon fat.

5. Pour the remaining 1 litre vegetable oil into a deep saucepan (at least 2 litres in capacity) and set over a medium-high heat. When the oil reaches 180°C on a thermometer, deep-fry the reserved bacon rinds until the bubbles stop emerging from the rinds, then continue frying for just a few minutes more, about 8 minutes in total. Remove with a slotted spoon and drain thoroughly on kitchen paper. The rinds should be crisp and light.

6. For the ramen, bring the Cream Tare to a simmer in a small saucepan over a medium heat, stirring frequently. Place the freshly cooked noodles and hot Cream Tare in a warmed mixing bowl along with all the remaining ramen ingredients and mix well. Serve in a hot serving bowl with all the toppings.

In the Bone Daddies Kitchen:
Making our confit duck leg

Duck Aburamen

At our sister restaurant Flesh & Buns we confit a lot of duck and so have loads of duck fat spare. We hate wasting anything and see an excess of something as a challenge to invent a dish to use it up. The *abura* (fatty) style is thought to have started as cheap 'staff food' in Japan – basically, ramen restaurants always have fat so ramen + fat + tare + spring onions = staff food and *aburamen* was born. Ours goes a bit further, of course, and has crispy duck bits.

Confit Duck Leg (makes enough for 4 servings)
4 duck legs
8 tablespoons rock salt
250g duck fat, or vegetable oil

Aburaman (per serving)
100g Confit Duck Leg meat and skin (see above)
60ml (4 tablespoons) duck fat, reserved from making the Confit Duck Leg (see above)

100g Tokyo wavy noodles, cooked (see page 117)
2 tablespoons Soy Tare (see page 108)

To Serve (per serving)
30g Pickled Shishito Peppers (see page 27)
50g Sliced Spring Onions (see page 118)
small handful of mustard leaves

The reserved duck fat has a long shelf life and can be used over and over again.

1. To make the Confit Duck Leg, cover the duck legs on all sides with the rock salt and leave in the refrigerator for 3 hours. Carefully wash each duck leg under cold running water to remove the excess salt, then dry thoroughly with kitchen paper.

2. Preheat the oven to 120°C/Gas Mark ½. Place the legs and duck fat (or oil) in an ovenproof dish, cover with foil and cook for 3 hours, or until the meat comes away easily from the bone.

3. Remove from the oven and leave to cool to room temperature in the fat, then carefully remove any bone and cartilage, reserving the fat and skin. Cover and chill in the refrigerator.

4. Once cold, cut or pull the duck leg meat and skin into 3cm pieces. Melt, strain and reserve the duck fat (see Tip).

5. Just before serving, fry the duck pieces in a frying pan in the reserved duck fat until golden and crisp, concentrating most of the cooking on the skin side.

6. Add the hot noodles and Soy Tare to a hot mixing bowl and mix together very well. Add the duck and mix roughly, them transfer to a hot serving plate or bowl.

7. Top with the Pickled Shishito Peppers, Sliced Spring Onion and mustard leaves, and serve immediately.

4
Sweet Stuff
& Drinks

Ice Cream

We opened without a single dessert on the menu and a lot of people asked for something sweet, so we wondered what could we do out of our little kitchen. We thought about trips to Japan and Lawson supermarkets with their Mr Whippy, or Whippy-san, soft-serve machines with green tea ice cream in them. Who doesn't love the texture of soft-serve ice cream? So we bought a machine and went on the soft serve-making adventure. We know that a soft-serve machine isn't a typical piece of kitchen kit, but these recipes all work well for normal ice cream too.

Makes about 1.3 litres

800ml whole milk
200g double cream
80g Inverted Sugar Syrup
(either store-bought or
see recipe, right)

6 large egg yolks, beaten
until liquid
60g caster sugar

**Inverted Sugar Syrup
(Makes 550ml)**

500g caster sugar
tiny pinch of cream
of tartar

1. To make the Inverted Sugar Syrup (if making) have a heatproof pastry brush ready in a small bowl of cold water. Put the sugar and cream of tartar in a saucepan with 240ml of water and stir to partially dissolve the sugar. Place over a very low heat and continue to stir until the sugar has dissolved completely, then stop stirring (otherwise the sugar will crystallize and make the syrup cloudy and coarse).

2. Increase the heat and bring the syrup to the boil, washing any sugar crystals at the edge of the pan down with the pastry brush dipped in cold water. Continue to simmer briskly until the temperature reaches 114°C on a thermometer. Cover the pan with a lid, remove from the heat and leave to cool completely. The syrup will keep in an airtight container in the refrigerator for at least 6 months.

3. To make the ice cream, bring the milk, cream and Inverted Sugar Syrup to the boil in a large saucepan, then reduce the heat.

4. Whisk the egg yolks and caster sugar together in a bowl until pale and fluffy. Add a ladleful of the hot milk mixture and whisk to combine. Then add all the egg mixture to the pan containing the remaining milk mixture and cook over a low heat, stirring continuously, until the custard is thick enough to coat the back of a spoon.

5. Quickly strain the custard through a fine-mesh sieve into a bowl over ice, stirring to speed up the cooling process.

6. Once the custard has cooled, add a little of it to your chosen flavouring (see page 222) in a separate bowl and whisk to a smooth paste. Return the paste to the remaining ice cream custard and whisk until incorporated.

7. Strain the mixture through a fine-mesh sieve to ensure there are no lumps. The mixture is now ready to be churned, either by hand or in an ice-cream machine according to the manufacturer's instructions.

Ice Cream Flavours

Now you've got your basic ice-cream recipe, mix it up with some of the following flavours.

Green Tea

The classic flavour of Japan.

```
15g green tea - we use funmatsu sencha because
of its bright green colour and taste
```

Black Sesame

We crush our own sesame seeds to make the paste. The paste tastes amazing and the ice cream tastes even better.

```
100g black sesame paste - make your own by toasting
black sesame seeds in a dry frying pan and then
grinding to a paste in a powerful food processor
(the seeds should release enough oil to form a paste),
but it's fine to use shop-bought Japanese sesame paste
(atari goma), just make sure it's a black variety
before you buy it.
```

Kinako

Used a lot in Japanese pastry, kinako is a roasted soya bean powder. The best way we could come up with to describe the taste is that it is a bit like a cheap ice-cream cone but more delicious.

```
25g kinako (roasted soya bean powder)
```

There are loads of different flavours that you can try in addition to these. For Ginger, for example, blitz 75g Chinese stem ginger and 50g of its syrup together. Experiment and see what takes your fancy.

Sugared Almonds

Graham Cracker

Salted Sesame Snaps

Ice Cream Toppings

Graham Cracker

Used as a topping for the salty taste and texture it adds to the ice cream; it works with all flavours of ice cream.

Makes 1.1kg mix or about 600g cooked crackers

250g wholemeal plain flour
190g white plain flour
125g dark soft brown sugar
a pinch fine sea salt

4g (1 scant teaspoon) baking powder
2.5g (½ teaspoon) bicarbonate of soda
250g unsalted butter, melted

1 vanilla pod, split lengthways and seeds scraped out
125g honey
125ml milk

1. Preheat the oven to 170°C/Gas Mark 3½.

2. Mix the flours, sugar, salt, baking powder and bicarbonate of soda together in a bowl with a whisk. Add the melted butter and vanilla seeds and mix to a wet sandy texture.

3. Add the honey and milk and mix to a dough – it will be very wet. Cover the bowl with cling film and leave to rest in the refrigerator for 30 minutes.

4. Roll out one-quarter of the dough between 2 sheets of nonstick baking paper to a rectangle about 3mm thick as evenly as possible. Remove the top sheet of paper and transfer the cracker on the bottom sheet to a large baking sheet (you will need 2 baking sheets to bake all 4 sheets of dough).

5. Repeat with the remaining mixture.

6. Bake the crackers for 9 minutes, then check them for doneness – they should be golden and crisp. If necessary, bake for a further 2–3 minutes. Leave to cool on the baking sheets for 5 minutes, then transfer to a wire rack to cool completely. The crackers can then be used on ice cream, or as a base for Soft Graham Crumble (see below).

Soft Graham Crumble

Makes about 350g

190g Graham Cracker (see above), crushed into small pieces

20g milk powder
25g caster sugar
3g (½ teaspoon) Maldon sea salt, finely crushed

55g unsalted butter, melted
55g double cream

1. Preheat the oven to 160°C/Gas Mark 3.

2. Mix the Graham Cracker pieces, milk powder, sugar and salt together in a bowl.

3. In a separate bowl, mix the melted butter and cream together, then add to the dry ingredients. Gently mix together to form crumbs.

4. Spread out on a baking sheet and bake for 5–10 minutes, stirring at frequent intervals, until slightly crisp.

Salted Sesame Snaps

Sesame brittle. What's not to like?

Makes about 200g

150g caster sugar
50g glucose syrup
350g black or white
sesame seeds

5g Maldon sea salt,
crushed
a little sunflower or other
flavourless oil

1. Heat the sugar, glucose syrup and 2 tablespoons of water in a large saucepan, stirring occasionally with a small metal whisk – try not to get sugar on the sides of the pan – until the sugar has melted. Once melted, continue to heat the mixture until it is smooth and golden.

2. Add the sesame seeds and salt, then reduce the heat and stir with a wooden spoon to coat the seeds thoroughly with the caramel.

3. Spread the mixture over a clean, lightly oiled surface or baking tray. Leave to cool, then crush into 1–2cm chunks.

Ginger Graham Crumble

Makes about 450g

300g Graham Cracker (see
right), crushed into small
pieces
30g milk powder
40g caster sugar

4g Maldon sea salt
15g ground ginger
85g unsalted butter,
melted
85g double cream

1. Preheat the oven to 160°C/Gas Mark 3.

2. Mix the Graham Cracker pieces, milk powder, sugar, salt and ginger together in a bowl.

3. In a separate bowl, mix the melted butter and cream together, then add to the dry ingredients. Gently mix together and the mixture should form crumbs.

4. Spread out on a baking sheet and bake for 10–20 minutes, stirring at frequent intervals, until evenly golden.

SunGae

A Soho sundae. Our manager suggested the name and it just stuck.

Serves 1 generously

200g ice cream (about 4 x 50g scoops), softened

60ml (4 tablespoons) raspberry purée – we use Boiron

15g Ginger Graham Crumble (see page 225)

15g Soft Graham Crumble (see page 224)

handful of mixed berries

30g Sugared Almonds (see below)

15g honeycomb, roughly crushed

1. Layer the ice cream and raspberry purée in a tall half-pint (285ml) glass.

2. Top with the Crumbles, berries, Sugared Almonds and honeycomb.

Sugared Almonds

Just a tasty little topping. Nuff said!

Makes about 215g

150g flaked almonds

1 large egg white, lightly beaten

75g icing sugar, sifted

a little sunflower or other flavourless oil, for oiling

1. Preheat the oven to 160°C/Gas Mark 3.

2. Put the almonds in a bowl. Mix the egg white into the almonds to coat them evenly. Slowly mix in the icing sugar until evenly coated again.

3. Place on an oiled tray and bake for about 15 minutes, checking and stirring at 5-minute intervals, until golden brown throughout.

Hard Shakes

This was obvious – we had a machine that was making more than 50 per cent of what we needed to make boozy milkshakes, the rest is history. We would hate to have to pick a favourite.

Makes 1

75ml milk
300g Ice Cream (see pages 221–22)
50ml of your chosen spirit

1. Place all the ingredients in a blender and blitz for a few seconds. Pour into a tall glass.

Shake flavours that we like include Stem Ginger or Black Sesame Ice Cream with dark rum (we use Gosling's Black Seal rum), and Green Tea or Kinako Ice Cream with whisky (preferably Nikka All Malt whisky).

Stem Ginger
& Dark Rum

Black Sesame
& Dark Rum

Kinako &
Whisky

Green Tea &
Whisky

Orenji
What?!

Mr Sparkle

Ginger Sour

Frozen Yuzu
Margarita

Soft Cocktail

Mocktails and Cocktails

Our cocktail names are normally a team effort, as we encourage the guys to come up with suggestions. We have had some great ones over the years. We have had some shit ones also. All recipes make 1, unless otherwise stated.

Soft Cocktail

There was a period of time when all suggestions for cocktail names had sex references. It was just the personalities in the team we had at the time, and this name slipped through. Shit name, great drink. Calpico is a strange little drink, but we like to use it.

```
75ml watermelon juice
50ml apple juice
25ml lime juice
25ml Calpico
lime wedge, to garnish
```

1. Put some ice in a highball glass. Add all the ingredients to a cocktail shaker with ice. Shake together and strain into the glass. Garnish with a lime wedge and serve with a straw.

Orenji What?!

This has orange in it, which is *orenji* in Japanese, so we wanted to call it *Orenji* Something and imagined the exchange between the barman and a customer in a loud bar if this were ordered... so Orenji What?! it is.

```
50ml bourbon, ideally Evan Williams
10ml triple sec
20ml orange juice
20ml sugar syrup
15ml water
2 dashes Angostura bitters
strip of orange peel, to garnish
```

1. Put some ice in a martini glass. Add all the ingredients to a cocktail shaker with ice. Shake together and strain into the glass. Garnish with the orange peel to serve.

Mr Sparkle

This was named after *The Simpsons* episode where Homer thinks his face has been used as the logo for a Japanese dishwasher detergent called Mr Sparkle.

```
100ml pink grapefruit and cucumber juice
15ml lemon juice
15ml oolong syrup
soda water, to top up (about 90ml)
grapefruit twist, to garnish
```

1. Add the juices and oolong syrup to a highball glass. Fill up with ice and stir, then top up with soda water. Garnish with a grapefruit twist and serve with a straw.

Ginger Sour

Sours are a favourite drink of ours: they go down dangerously easily. Try a few of these if you think you are getting a cold. It could be a cure.

```
50ml Lemon Grass & Ginger Sake
(see page 246)
20ml sugar syrup
5ml ginger juice
25ml Chivas Regal whisky
25ml lemon juice
1 egg white
2 dashes of Angostura bitters
slice of lemon, to garnish
stem of lemon grass, to garnish
```

1. Add all the ingredients to a cocktail shaker and shake well. Add ice to the cocktail shaker and shake again. Strain into a rocks glass over ice and garnish with a lemon slice and a stem of lemon grass.

Frozen Yuzu Margarita

When Ross moved to Texas, he realized how good a margarita could actually be and wanted to have one in our first restaurant. It obviously needed a Japanese element to fit, so we use loads of great-quality yuzu juice to make this recipe. We now have a frozen margarita machine in all our restaurants and this recipe has become a staple.

Makes about 2 litres

```
lime wedges, to garnish
Maldon sea salt, to garnish
large quantity of crushed ice
175ml tequila
100ml triple sec
125ml yuzu juice
60ml agave syrup
50ml sugar syrup
125ml lime juice
```

1. First, prepare rocks glasses for serving by rubbing the rim of each with a lime wedge, then turning in a saucer of sea salt to coat.

2. Fill a large blender (or prepare in batches if your blender is too small) with as much crushed ice as you like (depending on how strong you want the Margarita to be), add all the ingredients and blend thoroughly.

3. Pour the frozen mixture into the prepared glasses and garnish each with a lime wedge.

Berry Berry Nice

Watermelon Crush

Watermelon Crush

On the farm where Ross grew up, there was a field where they grew watermelons to sell to market and one year there were so many that they couldn't pick them all. Watermelons get so ripe and delicious in the baking Queensland sun, but they also over-ripen and ferment very quickly. When they let the dairy cows in to finish the last of the melons, they got completely pissed and were falling over – you will, too, if you drink too many of these.

```
50ml shōchū
50ml watermelon juice
25ml yuzu shu
20ml lime juice
15ml sugar syrup
watermelon wedge,
to garnish
```

1. Put some ice in a rocks glass. Add all the ingredients to a cocktail shaker with ice. Shake together and strain into the glass. Garnish with a watermelon wedge.

Berry Berry Nice

We fucking hate this name and don't know how it got this far. The name will have been changed before you read this.

```
20ml raspberry purée
10ml yuzu juice
5ml sugar syrup
50ml gin
ginger beer, to top up
1 raspberry, to garnish
```

1. Add all the ingredients except the ginger beer to a rocks glass. Add ice and top up with ginger beer. Stir and garnish with a raspberry to serve.

Lychee Saketini

BD Fruity

Unnamed

Plumbob

Oishi Mofo

Chuhai 1

Plumbob

Plum has worked with us since day one and is a great part of our team. She made it, so it's named after her. Thanks Plum!

```
50ml ume shu
125ml prosecco
2 dashes of orange bitters
twist of orange peel, to garnish
```

1. Fill a wine glass with ice. Add the ume shu, top up with the prosecco and add the bitters. Garnish with a twist of orange peel and serve with a straw.

BD Fruity

Bone Daddies' Fruity has been a staple since we opened.

```
1 passion fruit
about 5 mint leaves, plus an extra mint
sprig to garnish
15ml passion fruit syrup
orange juice, to top up (about 150ml)
```

1. Cut the passion fruit in half and scoop out the seeds and pulp into a highball glass. Clap the leaves between your hands to release the flavour, then add to the glass with the passion fruit syrup. Fill with up ice, then top up with orange juice. Stir. Garnish with a sprig of mint and serve with a straw.

Chuhai 1

A chuhai is a very common alcoholic drink in Japan, the basic kind involving shōchū, carbonated water and lemon juice – you can even buy it in a can. This is our version, taking it a bit further.

```
50ml pear purée
50ml shōchū
15ml sugar syrup
15ml lemon juice
soda water, to top up
apple slices, to garnish
```

1. Build the pear purée, shōchū, sugar syrup and lemon juice in highball glass and stir. Fill with ice and top up with soda water. Garnish with apple slices and serve with a straw.

Oishi Mofo

Oishi is what is said in Japanese when something is delicious. And 'mofo' we all know!

```
50ml White Tea-infused Sake (see below)
25ml mugi (barley) shōchū
25ml yuzu shu
15ml maple syrup
2 dashes of orange bitters
shiso cress, to garnish
```

White Tea-infused Sake
```
50g whole leaf white tea (we get ours
from the Rare Tea Company)
1.8-litre bottle sake
```

1. To make the White Tea-infused Sake, infuse the white tea in the bottle of sake overnight, then strain through a fine-mesh sieve to remove the tea. Build all the cocktail ingredients in a rocks glass and fill with ice. Garnish with shiso cress.

Lychee Saketini

It's all in the name.

```
50ml lychee sake
25ml vodka
30ml lychee syrup, from canned lychees
1 lychee (from lychee sake if liked),
to garnish
```

1. Add all the ingredients to a cocktail shaker with ice. Shake together and strain, then strain again into a martini glass. Garnish with a lychee.

Unnamed

Literally, the drink was ready but the name was not.

```
45ml whisky, ideally  Nikka All Malt
15ml ume shu
15ml Pink Peppercorn and Vanilla Syrup
(see below), strained
2 dashes of Angostura bitters
2 dashes of peach bitters
twist of lemon peel, to garnish
```

Pink Peppercorn and Vanilla Syrup (makes about 500ml)
```
20 pink peppercorns, lightly crushed
2 vanilla pods, split lengthways
360g caster sugar
500ml hot water
```

1. To make the Pink Peppercorn and Vanilla Syrup, add all the ingredients to a sterilized jar and stir until fully mixed. Leave with the lid off to cool completely, then seal with the lid and store in a cool, dark place for up 6 months.

2. To make the cocktail, add all the ingredients to a rocks glass with ice, stir and garnish with lemon peel.

Gini Hendrix

The team was having a bit of fun with the name of this one. It works because classic rock and roll is part of our brand and experience.

Oolong Syrup (makes 700ml)
1 x 50g packed oolong tea leaves
700g granulated sugar
700ml hot water

Gini Hendrix
1cm peeled and deseeded piece cucumber
35ml Tanqueray gin
15ml oolong syrup
25ml yuzu shu
10ml yuzu juice
50ml soda water, to top up
cucumber strip, to garnish

1. To make the Oolong Syrup, add the ingredients in the order above to a sterilised jar. Stir until fully mixed. Leave to cool and infuse for at least 1 day. Strain and seal until ready for use. This will keep in a cool dark place for up to 2 months.

2. To make the Gini Hendrix, muddle the cucumber with the gin in a highball glass. Add the oolong syrup, yuzu shu and yuzu juice, them some ice, top with the soda water and stir well. Garnish with a cucumber strip and serve with a straw.

Bloody Good
Mary

Tokyo Mule

S&M

Chuhai 2

Shogun's Glory

Shogun's Glory

It's quite a boozy drink this, so we imagined it's something that Shoguns would drink: a fighting punch for heading off to battle.

```
50ml apple juice
25ml triple sec
25ml whisky
25ml vodka
25ml lime juice
10ml Calpico
apple slice, to garnish
```

1. Put some ice in a highball glass Add all the ingredients to a cocktail shaker with ice. Shake together and strain into the glass. Garnish with an apple slice and serve with a straw.

Tokyo Mule

Like a traditional Moscow Mule, but tickled a bit differently.

```
25ml shōchū
25ml dark rum
15ml yuzu juice
½ lime, cut into wedges, plus lime wheel,
to garnish
2 dashes of Angostura bitters
ginger beer, to top up (about 100ml)
```

1. Add all the ingredients except the ginger beer to a highball glass. Fill with ice and top up with ginger beer. Stir and then garnish with a lime wheel and serve with a straw.

Bloody Good Mary

A Sunday fix-you-up. This and a bowl of ramen will cure the mother of all hangovers.

```
50ml vodka
20ml Bloody Mary Mix (see below)
130ml tomato juice
large shiso leaf, to garnish
```

Bloody Mary Mix (makes about 300ml)
```
200g roasted cherry tomatoes, skinned
95ml Worcestershire sauce
40ml sriracha sauce
50ml soy sauce
½ barspoon Kimchi Tare (see page 112)
```

1. To make the Bloody Mary Mix, blend the cherry tomatoes in a food processor or blender to a smooth paste. Add to the other ingredients and mix well. Add the vodka and Bloody Mary mix to a highball glass, fill with ice and top up with the tomato juice, then stir. Garnish with a large shiso leaf and serve with a straw.

S&M

Strawberry and mint combined with our twisted little minds gives way to this summery beverage.

```
25ml strawberry purée
20ml lemon juice
10ml sugar syrup
about 5 mint leaves, plus an extra sprig
to garnish
soda water, to top up
```

1. Add the strawberry purée, lemon juice, sugar syrup and mint leaves to a highball glass with a handful of ice. Top up with soda water and stir. Garnish with a sprig of mint and serve with a straw.

Chuhai 2

Just the second Chuhai that we created...

```
1 passion fruit
25ml mango purée
25ml passion fruit purée
50ml shōchū
15ml sugar syrup
soda water, to top up (about 90ml)
```

1. Set aside one-quarter of the passion fruit for garnish. Scoop out the seeds and pulp of the remaining three-quarters into a highball glass and add the fruit purées, shochu and sugar syrup. Fill with ice, top up with soda water and stir. Garnish with the reserved passion fruit quarter and serve with a straw.

Flavoured Sakes and Shōchū

These are easy ways to introduce people to the great drinks of Japan, sake and shōchū. They are very simple to make, they just take a bit of time to infuse. If anyone says they do not like sake or shōchū, give them some of these to try. We could drink them all night!

We serve 100ml shōchū over 4–5 ice cubes, and serve sake neat in a 150ml carafe, which is then poured into a large shot glass. Each of these infusions should keep well for up to a year if you store them in an airtight jar in a cool, dark place.

Lemon Grass & Ginger Sake

Makes 1.8 litres

20 stems of lemon grass, finely chopped and crushed
500g fresh root ginger, peeled and roughly chopped
1.8-litre bottle of sake

1. Combine all the ingredients in a very large sterilized storage jar, or divide between smaller jars, and leave to infuse in a cool, dark place for 1 week. Strain to remove the lemon grass and ginger before using. Return to the airtight jar or jars to store as previously.

Passion Fruit Sake

Makes 1.8 litres

20 passion fruits, halved and seeds and pulp scooped out
1.8-litre bottle of sake
caster sugar, to taste (optional)

1. Combine the passion fruits and sake in a very large sterilized storage jar, or divide between smaller jars, and leave to infuse in a cool, dark place for at least 3 days. Strain, then taste the sake from the jar and add sugar if needed to suit your taste. Return to the airtight jar or jars to store as previously.

Lychee Sake

Makes 1.8 litres

2 x 567g cans of lychees, strained
1.8-litre bottle of sake

1. Combine both the ingredients in a very large sterilized storage jar, or divide between smaller jars, and leave to infuse in a cool, dark place for at least 3 days. Strain before using. Return to the airtight jar or jars to store as previously.

Date Sake

Makes 1.8 litres

1kg fresh dates, pitted and quartered
1.8-litre bottle of sake

1. Combine both the ingredients in a very large sterilized storage jar, or divide between smaller jars, and leave to infuse in a cool, dark place for at least 3 days. Strain before using. Return to the airtight jar or jars to store as previously.

Mango Shōchū

Makes 1.4 litres

6 mangoes, bought 3 at
a time, 1-2 weeks apart
2 x 720ml bottles
of shōchū
caster sugar, to taste
(optional)

1. Stone, peel and cut up the first batch of 3 mangoes and add to a large sterilized storage jar with the shochu. Leave to infuse in a cool, dark place for about 1–2 weeks, tasting regularly to ensure that the shōchū is taking on the mango flavour.

2. Once the shōchū has taken on some of the yellow colour of the mangoes, strain and discard the fruit. Prepare the second batch of 3 mangoes and add to the shōchū in the jar, then leave to infuse for about 1 week. Strain again and add sugar to taste if you like it extra sweet. Return to the airtight jar to store as previously.

Coffee Shōchū

Makes 1.4 litres

2 x 720ml bottles
of shōchū
500g fresh roasted coffee
beans
caster sugar, to taste

1. Add the shōchū and coffee beans to a large sterilized storage jar and leave to infuse in a cool, dark place for 1 week. Strain, then taste the shōchū from the jar and add sugar if needed to suit your taste.

Mandarin Shōchū

Makes 1.4 litres

2 x 720ml bottles
of shōchū
10 mandarins, peeled and
segmented
caster sugar, to taste

1. Add the shōchū and mandarin segments to a large
sterilized storage jar and leave to infuse in a cool, dark place
for 1 week. Strain, then taste the shōchū from the jar and add
sugar if needed to suit your taste.

Strawberry Shōchū

Makes 1.4 litres

2 x 720ml bottles of shōchū
1kg fresh strawberries, hulled
and quartered
caster sugar, to taste

1. Add the shōchū and strawberries to a large sterilized
storage jar and leave to infuse in a cool, dark place for 3
days. Strain, then taste the shōchū from the jar and add
sugar if needed to suit your taste.

Index

Index

Index

Acknowledgements

Ross Shonhan

Making everything for a bowl of ramen initially seems quite easy but it takes time, patience and a lot of hard work; I can say now that is not unlike creating a cookbook.

I would like to thank Stephanie Jackson at Octopus and Cathryn Summerhayes at William Morris for gently pushing me over the years until I finally say yes to do this book. Hopefully your persistence has paid off.

We have to thank our loyal customers who have become fans of what we do because without your support we would not have our restaurants or this book. We are continually humbled by your custom.

To my business partners, especially Bernard Kantor, who believed in me when Bone Daddies was an idea and they had no clue what ramen was but backed me anyway.

To Dinah Meister and our teams who continually make sure the cogs are turning to ensure all our restaurants run as well and as smoothly as they do.

I definitely need to thank Tom Moxon for his dedication to Bone Daddies and for this this book that he helped to bring to life.

To my family back home in Australia, who I struggle to get home to visit often enough but who I know are my biggest supporters.

Finally, to my lady Vivien who knows what it's like running a business and whose patience, thoughtfulness and love is a constant source of strength.

Tom Moxon

I would like to thank Loic Leguay for his invaluable input during the photo shoot and for blitzing the pork stock for longer than was truly necessary.

Fran Astbury and Brit Stark for doing a fantastic job at the drinks photo shoot and for answering our many many questions.

Thanks to Ross for continued guidance and for always believing in me.

To everyone at Bone Daddies, past and present, for their roles in the adventure so far and in making Bone Daddies what it is today.

To Stephanie, Pauline and Juliette at Octopus Publishing for their seemingly boundless enthusiasm, experience and patience.

And a special thank you to Mum and Dad for always being the definition of selfless and for instilling in me a curiosity in all things.

Picture Acknowledgements

Alamy AF Archive 32, 38-39; Enrique de Sequera 90; J Marshall - Tribaleye Images 58, 166-167; Matthew Ashton 132; Mattias Helgesson 163. **Bridgeman Images** Pictures from History 176. **Courtesy of Asahi Breweries** 174, 223, 224. **Dreamstime.com** Bidouze Stéphane 129. **Getty Images** Buyenlarge 178; Dan Higham 103. iStock Cristian Baitg 104; Starcevic 244-245. **Poster art by Patryk Czajkowski** 255. **REX Shutterstock** Austral Int. 50, 56-57; Patrick Frilet 108; T-LINK/Ayano Sato 74. **The Kobal Collection** Sedic/RPC/Dentsu 6; Shochiku 12; Toho 11, 19.

This book has been created in the
traditional Japanese style to be
read from right to left.

Please flip the book over and
start at the other end.